THE VIKING RUNES *Traditional Meanings*

Rune	Name	Meaning
ᛗ	the Self	Man, the Human Race
X	Partnership	A gift, Offerings from the gods or from Chiefs to Loyal Followers
ᚠ	Signals	God, the god Loki, Mouth (source of Divine Utterances), Rivermouth
◊	Retreat	Property or Inherited Possessions, also Native Land, Home
ᚢ	Strength	Strength, Sacrificial Animal, the Aurochs (*bos primigenius*), species of wild ox
ᚲ	Initiation	Uncertain Meaning, a Secret Matter (Rune of Mystery)
ᚾ	Constraint	Need, Necessity, Constraint, Cause of Human Sorrow, Lessons, Hardship
ᛜ	Fertility	Ing, the Legendary Hero, later a god
ᛇ	Defense	Yew-tree, a Bow Made of Yew, Rune Magic, Avertive Powers: Runic Calendars or "Primstaves"
ᛉ	Protection	Protection, Defense, the Elk, Sedge or Eelgrass
ᚹ	Possessions	Cattle, Goods, the Vital Community Wealth
ᚹ	Joy	Joy, also in *Cynewulf's* Runic Passages, Absence of Suffering & Sorrow
◇	Harvest	Year, Harvest, A Fruitful Year
ᚲ	Opening	Torch, Skiff, Ulcer, Associated with Cult of the Goddess Nerthus
↑	Warrior	Victory in Battle, a Guiding Planet or Star, the god Tiw
ᛒ	Growth	Birch Tree, Associated with Fertility Cults, Rebirth, New Life
M	Movement	Horse, Associated with the Course of the Sun
ᚱ	Flow	Water, Sea, a Fertility Source (See Grendel's Mere in *Beowulf*)
ᚻ	Disruption	Hail, Sleet, Natural Forces that Damage
R	Journey	A Riding, a Journey: Refers to the Soul After Death, Journey Charm
ᚦ	Gateway	Giant, Demon, Thorn, the god Thor
ᛞ	Breakthrough	Day, God's Light, Prosperity and Fruitfulness
ᛁ	Standstill	Ice, Freezing, in the *Prose Edda* the Frost-giant Ymir is Born of Ice
ᛋ	Wholeness	The Sun
☐	the unknowable	The Rune of Destiny

T
BOO
RU

The BOOK of RUNES

*A Handbook for the Use of
an Ancient Oracle:
The Viking Runes*

Commentary by
Ralph Blum

ORACLE BOOKS
ST. MARTIN'S PRESS
NEW YORK

Design by Deborah Daly
Edited by Bronwyn Jones
Ilustrations by Jancis Salerno

Library of Congress Cataloging-in-Publication Data

Blum, Ralph, 1932–
    The new book of runes.

    Rev. ed. of: The book of runes. c1982.
    Bibliography: p.
    1. Runes—Miscellanea. 2. Oracles. I. Blum, Ralph,
1932–   Book of runes. II. Title.
BF1779.R86B58 1987   133.3'3   87-13113
ISBN 0-312-00729-9

Third Edition

This book is lovingly dedicated
to
Margaret Mead

*To lend courage to virtue
and ardor to truth . . .*

—Dr. Samuel Johnson

CONTENTS

ACKNOWLEDGMENTS

For my introduction to the study of Oracles, I am indebted to Dr. Allan W. Anderson, Department of Religious Studies, San Diego State University. Dr. Anderson taught a unique course entitled "The Oracular Tradition," in which he presented the *I Ching* as "the only systematic sacred text we possess." His scholarship, his presentation of seminal concepts, and his creative influence encouraged me to persevere in my study of "the finest art of all—the art of self-change."

I am especially grateful to Murray Hope who, on a rainy Wednesday afternoon, in Redhill, Surrey, England, introduced me to the Runes as a contemporary Oracle.

My first attempts at writing this handbook for the use of the Runes as a personal Oracle included an additional seventy-three pages of history, philology, and archeology. For support and encouragement in reducing the text to this more concise and manageable form, I gratefully thank my friend and editor, Bronwyn Jones.

Finally, my sincere thanks to my editor at St. Martin's Press, Tom Dunne, who has been unstintingly generous in encouraging me to introduce new insights and techniques into the original text.

PREFACE

The Runes as described here are healing, merciful Runes; they will do you no harm. Learn their language and let them speak to you. Play with the possibility that they can provide "a mirror for the magic of our Knowing Selves," a means of communication with the knowledge of our subconscious minds.

Remember that you are consulting an Oracle rather than having your fortune told. An Oracle does not give you instruction as to what to do next, nor does it predict future events. An Oracle points your attention towards those hidden fears and motivations that will shape your future by their unfelt presence within each present moment. Once seen and recognized, these elements become absorbed into the realm of choice. Oracles do not absolve you of the responsibility for selecting your future, but rather direct your attention towards those inner choices that may be the most important elements in determining that future.

How can random selection of marked stones tell you anything about yourself? Perhaps these Rune interpretations are simply so evocative that each contains *some* point which can be accepted as relevant to *some* part of what is happening at the limits of consciousness any day, any time, to anyone. That is the easiest possibility to accept from a strictly scientific standpoint. Nevertheless, my own play with these Runes has shown coincidence piled upon coincidence and an apparently consistent "appropriateness" in each Rune reading which is difficult to explain by the mechanism I have just described.

Can there be other factors that distort the expected randomness of Rune selection so as to provide a language by which the subconscious makes itself and its expectations known? For myself, I maintain an open mind, reminding myself that observations should not be discounted simply because their underlying mechanisms have not yet been satisfactorily explained.

So go ahead. Try out these Runes. See if this Oracle can mirror your subconscious process, but remember that such a link may take practice to develop. The Rune interpretations offered here come from the meditations of a gentle, healing mind. They will speak to you of change and growth. The only negativity you will find here relates to the blockage of appropriate growth, while all the positive aspects are transcendent, transforming and lead to breakthroughs. The subconscious you will encounter here is not a fearsome beast in need of obedience training. It is the inner seeker-after-truth who must be helped to save us from ourselves.

Dr. Martin D. Rayner
Professor of Physiology
University of Hawaii School of Medicine

Odin on the Yggdrasil,
or World Tree,
Spies the Runes

"THE SPEECH OF THE HIGH ONE"

I know I hung on that windswept tree,
Swung there for nine long nights,
Wounded by my own blade,
Bloodied for Odin,
Myself an offering to myself:
Bound to the tree
That no man knows
Whither the roots of it run.

None gave me bread,
None gave me drink.
Down to the deepest depths I peered
Until I spied the Runes.
With a roaring cry I seized them up,
Then dizzy and fainting, I fell.

Well-being I won
And wisdom too.
I grew and took joy in my growth:
From a word to a word
I was led to a word,
From a deed to another deed.

—From the Old Norse
The Poetic Edda (ca. A.D. 1200)

INTRODUCTION

Few people today have even heard the word "Runes." Among those of Scandinavian descent and among readers of Tolkien, yes, a light goes on. But that's about the extent of it. An ancient alphabetic script, each of whose letters possessed a meaningful name as well as a signifying sound, Runes were employed for poetry, for inscriptions and divination, yet never evolved as a spoken language. Next to nothing has been written about the Runes as a contemporary Oracle.

Both the alphabetical ordering and the letter interpretations found in *The Book of Runes* are non-conventional. The interpretations of the Runes as used for divination are lost to us. While *legomonism*—the passing on of sacred knowledge through initiation—was practiced among Rune Masters of old, their secrets were not recorded or, if recorded, did not survive. In ancient times, the Runes and their symbols were employed by warriors bent on conquest. It is my hope that the Runes, in their contemporary use, will serve the Spiritual Warrior, the one whose quest is doing battle with the self, the one whose goal is self-change. The *Bhagavad Gita* in Chapter 6, verse 5, says it succinctly:

> *Lift up the self by the Self*
> *And don't let the self droop down,*

*For the Self is the self's only friend
And the self is the Self's only foe.* *

The Book of Runes has been written as a handbook for the Spiritual Warrior. Free of anxiety, radically alone and unattached to outcomes, the Spiritual Warrior practices absolute trust in the struggle for awareness, and is constantly mindful that what matters is to have a *true present.* It takes a long time to grow in wisdom, to say nothing of the time it takes to learn to think well. Following the Warrior Way is not for everyone, although it is available to all who are willing to undergo its challenges. To embark on this path is to cultivate the Witness Self, the Watcher Within, the one who can profitably converse with the Runes.

Before beginning to write, I consulted the Runes about the timeliness of undertaking this work. The three Runes drawn were *Inguz* ⧓ , the Rune of Fertility and New Beginnings; *Nauthiz* ⇂ , the Rune of Necessity, Constraint and Pain; and *Dagaz* ⋈ , the Rune of Breakthrough and Transformation. *The Book of Runes* was conceived in one fertile sleepless night. The Constraint required during the long hours spent in editing and reworking the first half of the book was certainly not without pain. Yet through it all, I remained mindful of the French saying, "Pain is the craft entering into the apprentice." Working with the Runes has been a source of transformation in my own life and, through their

---

*Throughout *The Book of Runes,* the term *self* is used to represent the little self or ego-self, and *Self* to signify the Higher Self, the God Within.

introduction to the Runes, the lives of many others.

All along the way, since beginning this book, there have been positive signs and omens. The final sign came as I completed the Afterword. Since the last Rune Masters lived in seventeenth-century Iceland, it seemed to me fitting to close with an Icelandic blessing. In order to check the spelling of *Gud blessi thig,* the Icelandic for "God bless you," I placed a call to the Icelandic Consulate in New York. The woman who answered confirmed the spelling. When she heard about *The Book of Runes,* she paused a long moment, then said, "My name is Sigrun. It means 'Rune of Victory.' "

* * *

During the years since this book was first published, a number of new techniques have suggested themselves. Certain of these are now being included in this revised and expanded edition of *The Book of Runes.*

The *Five Rune Spread* (pp. 48) is helpful when you need to go deeply into an issue, to see it illuminated from several different perspectives. *Runes of Rectification, Water Runes,* and *Runes of Comfort for the Bereaved,* first presented in somewhat different form in *Rune Play* (St. Martin's Press, 1985), are here grouped in the chapter entitled Runecraft: Three New Spreads (pp. 63). *A Destiny Profile,* "a grid within which a human life can be framed," stands in a chapter on its own (pp. 70). For the many people who have written to ask about the pronunciation of the old Germanic Rune names, a Pronunciation Guide is included (pp. 146) in this new edition.

As time goes on, other techniques and practices

may be added to the original text. For, as *The Book of Runes* observes, "function determines form, use confirms meaning, and an Oracle always resonates to the requirements of the time in which it is consulted."

INVOCATION

God within me, God without,
How shall I ever be in doubt?
There is no place where I may go
And not there see God's face, not know
I am God's vision and God's ears.
So through the harvest of my years
I am the Sower and the Sown,
God's Self unfolding and God's own.

Rune stone, Västerby, Uppland, Sweden,
work of Asmund Karasun, *ca.* A.D. 1050

I

THE ORACLE
OF THE SELF

A King he was on a carven throne
In many-pillared halls of stone
With golden roof and silver floor,
And runes of power upon the door.

—J.R.R. Tolkien
The Fellowship of the Ring

Runes and charms are very practical formulae designed to produce
definite results, such as getting a cow out of a bog.

—T. S. Eliot
The Music of Poetry

The purpose of this book is to reintroduce an ancient Oracle, the Runes. Older than the New Testament, the Runes have lain fallow for more than 300 years. Akin in function to the Tarot and the Chinese *Book of Changes,* the Runes were last in current use in Iceland during the late Middle Ages. In their time they served as the *I Ching* of the Vikings.

The wisdom of the Rune Masters died with them. Nothing remains but the sagas, the far-flung fragments of runic lore and the Runes themselves. In his fine book, *Runes: An Introduction,* Ralph W.V. Elliott writes of

> strange symbols scratched into ancient tools and weapons now lying idle in some museum showcase; names of warriors, secret spells, even snatches of songs, appearing on objects as diverse as minute silver coins and towering stone crosses, scattered in the unlikeliest places from Yugoslavia to Orkney, from Greenland to Greece.*

The influence of the Runes on their time is incontestable. Elliott notes that when the high chieftains and wise counselors of Anglo-Saxon England met in conclave, they called their secret deliberations "runes," and that when Bishop Wulfila made his translation of the Bible into fourth-century Gothic, he rendered St. Mark's "the mystery of the kingdom of God" (Mark 4:11) using *runa* for "mystery." Eight centuries earlier, when the Greek historian Herodotus traveled around the Black Sea, he encountered descendants of Scythian tribesmen who crawled under blankets, smoked themselves into a stupor (a practice still encountered even today in the Caucasus Mountains) and then cast sticks in the air and "read" them when they fell. Although these tribesmen were preliterate, their sticks would probably qualify as Runes.

There is no firm agreement among scholars as to where and when runic writing first made its appearance

---

*Ralph W.V. Elliott, *Runes: An Introduction* (Manchester, Eng.: Manchester University Press, 1959), p. 1.

in Western Europe.* Before the Germanic peoples possessed any form of script, they used pictorial symbols that they scratched onto rocks. Especially common in Sweden, these prehistoric rock carvings or *hällristningar* are dated from the second Bronze Age (ca. 1300 B.C.), and were probably linked to Indo-European fertility and sun cults. The carvings include representations of men and animals, parts of the human body, weapon motifs, sun symbols, the swastika and variations on square and circular forms:

Elliott suggests an amalgamation of two separate traditions, "the alphabetic script on the one hand, the symbolic content on the other. . . . The practice of sortilege (divination) was cultivated among Northern Italic as well as Germanic peoples, the one using letters, the others pictorial symbols."† Numerous *hällristningar*, as well as the runic standing stones, can still be seen in the British Isles, in Germany, and throughout Scandinavia.

It is difficult for us to imagine the immense powers bestowed on the few who became skilled in the use of symbolic markings or glyphs to convey thought. Those

---

*Elliott writes: "All we know then is that in some Germanic tribe some man had both the leisure (a factor often forgotten) and the remarkable phonetic sense to catch the *futhark* (alphabetic script) from a North Italic model known to him somewhere in the alpine regions in the period *c.* 250–150 B.C." Op. cit., p. 11.

†Elliott, op. cit., pp. 64–5.

first glyphs were called *runes,* from the Gothic *runa,* meaning "a secret thing, a mystery." The runic letter, or *runastafr,* became a repository for intuitions that were enriched according to the skill of the practitioner of *runemal,* the art of Rune casting.

From the beginning, the Runes took on a ritual function, serving for the casting of lots, for divination and to evoke higher powers that could influence the lives and fortunes of the people. The craft of the runemal touched every aspect of life, from the most sacred to the most practical. There were Runes and spells to influence the weather, the tides, crops, love, healing; Runes of fertility, cursing and removing curses, birth and death. Runes were carved on amulets, drinking cups, battle spears, over the lintels of dwellings and onto the prows of Viking ships.

The Rune casters of the Teutons and Vikings wore startling garb that made them easily recognizable. Honored, welcomed, feared, these shamans were familiar figures in tribal circles. There is evidence that a fair number of runic practitioners were women. The anonymous author of the thirteenth-century *Saga of Erik the Red* provides a vivid description of a contemporary mistress of runecraft:

> She wore a cloak set with stones along the hem. Around her neck and covering her head she wore a hood lined with white catskins. In one hand she carried a staff with a knob on the end and at her belt, holding together her long dress, hung a charm pouch.

To pre-Christian eyes, the earth and all created things were alive. Twigs and stones served for runic divination since, as natural objects, they embodied sacred powers. Runic symbols were carved into pieces of hardwood, incised on metal or cut into leather that was then stained with pigment into which human blood was sometimes mixed to enhance the potency of the spell. The most common Runes were smooth flat pebbles with symbols or glyphs painted on one side. The practitioners of runemal would shake their pouch and scatter the pebbles on the ground; those falling with glyphs upward were then interpreted.

The most explicit surviving description of this procedure comes from the Roman historian Tacitus. Writing in A.D. 98 about practices prevalent among the Germanic tribes, he reports:

> To divination and casting of lots they pay attention beyond any other people. Their method of casting lots is a simple one: they cut a branch from a fruit-bearing tree and divide it into small pieces which they mark with certain distinctive signs *(notae)* and scatter at random onto a white cloth. Then, the priest of the community, if the lots are consulted publicly, or the father of the family, if it is done privately, after invoking the gods and with eyes raised to heaven, picks up three pieces, one at a time, and interprets them according to the signs previously marked upon them.
>
> *(Germania,* Ch. X)

By Tacitus' time, the Runes were already becoming widely known on the Continent. They were carried from place to place by traders, adventurers and warriors and, eventually, by Anglo-Saxon missionaries. For this to happen, a common alphabet was required—the alphabet that became known as *futhark* after its first six letters or glyphs:

f	u	th	a	r	k
ᚠ	ᚢ	ᚦ	ᚨ	ᚱ	ᚲ

Although later Anglo-Saxon alphabets expanded to include as many as thirty-three letters in Britain, the traditional Germanic futhark is comprised of twenty-four Runes. These were divided into three "families" of eight Runes, three and eight being numbers credited with special potency. The three groups, known as *aettir*, were named for the Norse gods *Freyr*, *Hagal* and *Tyr*. The three *aettir* are:

Freyr's Eight: ᚠ ᚢ ᚦ ᚨ ᚱ ᚲ ᚷ ᚹ

Hagal's Eight: ᚺ ᚾ ᛁ ᛃ ᛇ ᛈ ᛉ ᛊ

Tyr's Eight: ᛏ ᛒ ᛖ ᛗ ᛚ ᛜ ᛟ ᛞ

It is with these twenty-four Runes, plus one later innovation, a Blank Rune, that *The Book of Runes* is concerned.

THE RUNE OF HOSPITALITY

I saw a stranger yestereen;
I put food in the eating place,
  Drink in the drinking place,
  Music in the listening place;
And in the sacred names of the Triune
He blessed me and my house,
  My cattle and my dear ones.
And the lark said in her song:
  Often, often, often,
Goes the Christ in the stranger's guise:
  Often, often, often,
Goes the Christ in the stranger's guise.

—From the Gaelic

Christ figure, Jaellinge, Denmark, *ca.* A.D. 980

2

THE EMERGENCE
OF THE RUNES

oracle, *from the Latin* oraculum, *divine announcement . . . 1.*
among the ancient Greeks and Romans, a) the place where, or medium
by which, deities were consulted; b) the revelation or response of a
medium or priest; 2. a) any person or agency believed to be in communi-
cation with a deity; b) any person of great knowledge or wisdom; c)
opinions or statements of any such oracle; 3) the holy of holies of the
ancient Jewish Temple.

—Webster's New World Dictionary

And the oracle he prepared in the house within, to set there the ark of
the covenant of the Lord.

—I Kings 6:19

When I began to work with the Runes, I had never
seen a runic text and, therefore, did not realize that I
was breaking away from the traditional sequence of
Freyr, Hagal and Tyr used by the early practitioners of
runemal. But function determines form, use confers
meaning and an Oracle always resonates to the requirements of the time in which it is consulted. I had to rely
on the Runes to establish their own order and to in-
struct me in their meanings.

The Rune stones I was working with had come to me in England: tiny brown rectangles hardly bigger than a thumbnail, with the glyphs scratched into the surfaces. The woman who made them lived on Trindles Road, in the Surrey town of Redhill. She hadn't glazed her Runes, merely baked them in her oven like cookies.

Along with this set of Runes came two Xeroxed sheets giving the glyphs their approximate English meaning and a brief interpretation for each Rune when "Upright" or "Reversed." To the twenty-four original Runes had been added a Blank Rune represented simply as "The path of karma: That which is predestined and cannot be avoided. Matters hidden by the gods." There were no instructions for using the Runes and, after a few days, the Trindles Road Runes went onto a shelf.

But I kept the Runes and took them back to the United States. Several years passed before I happened upon them again. Alone on my Connecticut farm on a warm summer evening, unable to sleep, I went to my study and began rearranging books. And there, in their little chamois bag, were the Runes.

As I spilled the stones out onto my desk and moved them around, I experienced the same pleasurable feeling that I had when I first handled them in England. It was then that it occurred to me to ask the Runes how they were to be used. I sat quietly for a time, composing myself, and said a prayer. I opened my notebook and wrote out this question: "In what order do you wish to be arranged?" The time was 10:55 P.M., and the date, June 21st, the night of the summer solstice.

I spread out the Runes, blank sides up, and moved them around, touching each stone. Then, one by one, I turned them over, aligning them in front of me in three rows. It took only a few moments. When I was done, I sat and studied the arrangement:

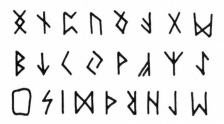

I remember my first feeling was dismay that the Blank Rune, the Rune of the Unknown, had not positioned itself more dramatically, rather than simply taking its place among the rest. And then I got an eerie feeling: The woman in England had said the Runes could be read *from right to left.* * Seen that way, the sequence began with the Rune of "The Self," *Mannaz* ⋈, and ended with the Blank Rune, the Rune that signals the presence of the Divine in our lives.

---

*The Runes could face either way and be read from left or right or, on occasion, vertically. Some inscriptions even read *boustrephedon,* from the Greek *bous,* an ox, and *strophe,* to turn, meaning the way an ox travels when plowing. See illustration on pp. 32.

It was while I sat gazing at the Rune of "The Self" that these words came to me:

The starting point is the self. Its essence is water. Only clarity, willingness to change, is effective now. . . .

The Viking Runes had begun their teaching.

I worked on through the night, taking each Rune in my hand, sitting with it, meditating on it, writing down what came to me. Now and then, when the flow dwindled, I turned to the *I Ching* and asked for a hexagram that would reveal the essence of a particular Rune. The spirit of some of those readings is incorporated into the interpretations of the Viking Runes. By the time I had completed the interpretation of the Blank Rune, the sun was rising.

Since that night, I have read a great deal about the Runes and their history, the controversies over their origins, the speculations concerning their use. Only one thing is certain: Beyond all the efforts of scholars to encompass them, the Runes remain elusive, for they are Odin's gift, and sacred.

Odin is the principal divinity in the pantheon of Norse gods. His name derives from the Old Norse for "wind" and "spirit," and it was through his passion, his transforming sacrifice of the self, that Odin brought us the Runes. According to legend, he hung for nine nights on the *Yggdrasil,* the Tree of the World, wounded by his own blade, tormented by hunger, thirst and pain, unaided and alone until, before he fell, he spied the Runes and, with a last tremendous effort, seized them.

Next to the gift of fire, that of the alphabet is the light in which we see our nature revealed. In *The Poetic Edda,* Odin, the great Rune Master, speaks across the centuries. Hear Odin now:

> Do you know how to cut them, know how to
> stain them,
> Know how to read them, how to understand?
> Do you know how to evoke them, know how to
> send them,
> Know how to offer, know how to ask?

> It is better not to offer than to offer too much
> for a gift demands a gift,
> Better not to slay than to slay too many.
> Thus did Odin speak before the earth began
> when he rose up in after time.

> These runes I know, unknown to kings' wives
> Or any earthly man. "Help" one is called,
> For help is its gift, and helped you will be
> In sickness and care and sorrow.

> Another I know, which all will need
> Who would study leechcraft.
> On the bark scratch them, on the bole of trees
> Whose boughs bend to the east.

I know a third—
If my need be great in battle
It dulls the swords of deadly foes,
Neither wiles nor weapons wound me
And I go all unscathed. . . .

So begins the sacred history of the Runes.

The motto for the Runes could be the same words that were carved above the gate of the Oracle at Delphi: *Know thyself.* The Runes are a teacher. Yet for some it may be more comfortable to approach the Runes in the spirit of play. Oracles are sacred games, instruments for serious or high play, and the value of play is that it frees us from the effort of learning, frees us to learn as children learn. *The Book of Runes* is offered as a primer for oracular play.

From this perspective, each of us is an Oracle. Consulting the Runes will put you in touch with your own inner guidance, with the part of you that knows everything you need to know for your life now.

If there is one prominent modern authority for the efficacy of Oracles, it is the Swiss psychologist Carl Jung, who affirmed that "theoretical considerations of cause and effect often look pale and dusty in comparison to the practical results of chance."[*] This suggests that nothing is too insignificant to be regarded as a clue to guide us in right and timely action. Consulting an Oracle places you in true present time because what-

[*]C.G. Jung, Foreword to the *I Ching* (Princeton, N.J.: Princeton University Press, 1950).

ever happens in the given moment possesses what Jung calls "the quality peculiar to that moment."

Experiencing a *true present* is something most of us find extremely difficult. We waste a good part of our lives dwelling on past regrets and fantasies of the future. In my own life, when I jog or drive long distances, I am often busy reviewing ideas, sorting schemes, going over options and opportunities. Suddenly I catch myself: I realize that miles of countryside have slipped by unseen, that I am not aware of breathing the air, not aware of the trees, the breeze, the ruts in the pavement. Nowadays, I catch myself more and more frequently, which is a beginning. The "roof-brain chatter" is slowly being replaced with a stillness that keeps me in the *now.* Once the momentum is broken, the habit will soon wither. I have only to remember: *In the spiritual life, we are always at the beginning.* Remembering this helps us to overcome our addiction to "getting ahead." For when we experience a true present, that is where everything happens.

Consulting the Runes enables you to bypass the strictures of reason, the fetters of conditioning and the momentum of habit.* For the brief span of interacting with the Runes you are declaring a free zone in which your life is malleable, vulnerable, and open to change. We are living in an age of radical discontinuity. The

---

*As Brugh Joy reminds us in his useful guidebook, *Joy's Way: A Map for the Transitional Journey,* there are three sets of mental fetters to give up if you want to be truly free: judging, comparing and needing to know why. The "why" inevitably becomes clear as you progress in your passage.

lessons come faster and faster as our souls and the universe push us into new growth. Familiar waters seem suddenly perilous, alive with uncharted shoals and shifting sandbars. The old maps are outdated; we require new navigational aids. And the inescapable fact is: *You are your own cartographer now.* Just as the Vikings used the information provided by the Rune Masters to navigate their ships under cloudy skies, so now you can use the Runes to modify your own life course. A shift of a few degrees at the beginning of any voyage will mean a vastly different position far out to sea.

Whatever the Runes may be—a bridge between the self and the Self, a link between the Self and the Divine, an ageless navigational aid—the energy that engages them is our own and, ultimately, the wisdom as well. Thus, as we start to make contact with our Knowing Selves, we will begin to hear messages of profound beauty and true usefulness. For like snowflakes and fingerprints, each of our oracular signatures is a one-of-a-kind aspect of Creation addressing its own.

CREDO

The truth is that life is hard and dangerous; that he who seeks his own happiness does not find it; that he who is weak must suffer; that he who demands love will be disappointed; that he who is greedy will not be fed; that he who seeks peace will find strife; that truth is only for the brave; that joy is only for him who does not fear to be alone; that life is only for the one who is not afraid to die.

—Joyce Cary

Boustrophedon script on stone
near Asferg, Sweden

3

CONSULTING
THE ORACLE

*The real voyage of discovery consists not in seeking new landscapes but
in having new eyes.*

—Marcel Proust

*Lord, grant me weak eyes for things that are of no account and strong
eyes for all thy truth.*

—Søren Kierkegaard

We walk by faith and not by sight.

—St. Paul

Once you start exploring the world of Runes, you
will discover that many people have developed their
own form of personal Rune casting. There is a man who
works the boardwalk in Venice, California. He sits on
an old sheet on which he has painted the rainbow circles of a bull's-eye. He has a bag of stones, shells and
twigs, and when you have posed your question he scat-
ters his "Runes" and reads from their spread. There are
people who work with sand dollars, bits of bone, stones
upon which they have scratched their own symbols.

Then there is what one of my friends calls "Noah Webster's Oracle." He opens the dictionary at random, taking his counsel from the words to which his finger points. At one moment, while working intensively on this book, I was presented with an attractive business opportunity that I felt obliged to pass up; in doing so, I feared I was missing out and I began giving myself a hard time. Instead of consulting the Runes on this issue, I opened a dictionary and, without looking, set my finger on the page. The counsel I received came under the words *lay off*, and contained, beneath my finger, the phrases "mark off boundaries . . . stop criticizing . . . minimize risk." I returned to the manuscript with a clear conscience.

Over the years, I have met a number of people who, without any precise knowledge of Oracles, employ the Bible in a similar fashion. It has long been my habit to consult the *Daily Word**** and attempt to live by its wisdom. It is a teacher for me, a monthly book of daily Oracles.

These contemporary Oracles, however homespun, are consistent with ancient traditions—such as the Chinese practice of reading oracle bones or the cracks that appear on tortoise shells when heated in a fire—and with the practice of *runemal* itself.

While working with the Runes, I have considered what, at its most basic, constitutes a Rune. At what

---

*An excellent collection of daily inspirational readings published monthly by Unity, Unity Village, Missouri 64065.

point is meaning present in a sign or glyph? Have you noticed the Warrior Rune ⇨ or ↑ on highways? Or the Rune of Opening Up ⟨ ... ⟨ ... ⟨ in a series at certain curves? Meaning is clearly present, agreed upon, but hardly oracular in nature—unless, of course, you happen to be mulling over an issue and see the sign at that moment, and it holds a special message for you.

I had a curious runic encounter in California while I was working on this book. One afternoon, driving to the beach for a counseling session, I took the Las Virgenes–Malibu Canyon Road, a beautiful drive across the mountains. Coming out of a curve, I looked across the canyon and there, on the mountainside opposite, someone had painted a Rune the height of a man. No question about it—I was looking up at *Algiz* ᛉ , the Rune of Protection. The glyph was painted on the rock face Reversed, a call for caution in the runic vocabulary. The artist had enclosed the Rune in a circle so that it appeared like this: ⊕. It took me a moment to realize that I was seeing a symbol from the antiwar movement of the 1960s. How curious that the protesters had settled on the Rune of Protection, probably without ever knowing it. I drove on, wondering whether, centuries from now, some zealous graduate student would attempt to prove that the Vikings had actually made it all the way to Malibu.

CONSULTING THE RUNES

There are people who set aside a special time each day at which to cast the Runes. Others prefer a more formal approach: lighting a candle, perhaps a stick of incense, taking time to compose themselves. Some find that meditation on the breath is helpful: Simply follow the breath in and out; let the breaths be long, easy, connected. Release all cares and concerns, if only for a moment. You may wish to say a prayer, especially if the situation confronting you is intense or turbulent.

Focus is important. But even if the ordinary business of living intrudes, you can always consult the Runes without formal preparation. Your need is what brings the Runes into play. And remember, you *are* in the realm of play, sacred play. A particularly good time to consult the Runes is when you have exhausted your own resources and are facing a situation about which you possess limited or incomplete information. Focus the issue clearly in your mind,* reach into your bag, make contact with the stones, and draw a Rune. As one practitioner of *runemal* put it, "The right Rune always sticks to my fingers."

When you cast the Runes for someone else, ask the person to formulate the matter of concern clearly in his mind but *not* state it aloud. This eliminates any uncon-

---

*"Just as in interpreting a dream, one must follow the dream text with utmost exactitude, so in consulting the oracle, one must hold in mind the form of the question put, for this sets a definite limit to the interpretation of the answer." C.G. Jung, op.cit., p.xxxvi.

scious personal bias in your interpretation of the Runes.

If a friend who lives far away could benefit from the perspective of a Rune reading, the telephone is your ally: Ask your friend to think of an issue, then draw a Rune from your bag. Rune reading works as well across 8,000 miles as it does face to face.

Should you wish to consult the Runes for another person and cannot ask his permission directly, it is best to ask the Oracle whether such action is timely and correct. Ask for a "Yes" or a "No" by reaching into your bag and drawing a Rune. Upright is "Yes," Reversed, "No." If you happen to draw one of the nine Runes which read the same Upright as well as Reversed, draw again.

APPROPRIATE ISSUES

An appropriate issue is *anything that relates to timeliness and right action.* You might wish advice on whether or not make a career change, sell a business, make an investment, move to a new home, terminate or initiate a relationship.

Notice that the word *issue* is used rather than *question.* A question might be, "Should I end the relationship?" To state it as an issue, you would say, "The issue is my relationship now." Instead of asking, "Should I accept this new job?" you might say, "The issue is my work." This small distinction is crucial. If you ask a question and the Oracle provides the answer, then your role is a passive one. However, if you present an issue, and the Oracle comments on that issue, this allows you to extract your own answer and to determine for yourself what is right action.

If you don't have a specific issue in mind, and still you feel drawn to consult the Runes, simply ask: *What do I need to know for my life now?* The Oracle's reply will always be instructive.

RUNIC OVERRIDE

Occasionally you may find that the counsel you receive doesn't seem to fit the issue posed. When this occurs, consider the possibility that the Runes have tuned in to a more significant issue, something you are avoiding, or something of which you are not consciously aware. This *runic override* seems to be an automatic fail-safe device. Similarly, if you find yourself caught between two issues and can't decide which one to address, don't worry, the Runes will select for you by addressing the issue of most immediate concern.

UPRIGHT AND REVERSED READINGS

Nine of the Runes read the same regardless of how you draw them from the bag. The other sixteen can be read either Upright or Reversed.

For example, the Rune of Movement, *Ehwaz*, Upright, looks like this: M , and Reversed, like this: W . The Reversed reading draws attention to aspects of a situation that might impede movement or to the fact that movement itself might be inappropriate at this time.

It is well to remember that the appearance of a Rune Reversed is not a cause for alarm but rather an indication that care and attention are required for your conduct to be correct. A Reversed reading often signals the presence of an opportunity to challenge some aspect of your behavior, some area in your life which, until now, you have been unwilling to face.

Whether you draw your Rune Upright or Reversed, it is always a good idea to read *both* aspects, as this will keep you in touch with the unseen side of your nature—that which is not presently being expressed. Reading both aspects of the Rune will help you to become more conscious of the forces of dark and light which combine to make up our natures.

CONSULTING TWO ORACLES

When you first start using the Runes, you may want to check them for accuracy, in effect to calibrate them. This can be done by consulting two different oracular instruments on the same issue.

When I began working with the Runes, in order to confirm their responses with those of a known and wise friend, I would often address the same issue both to the *I Ching* and to the Runes. Time after time, I found the two Oracles to be in accord, sometimes identical in their symbolic content, often complementary, always a mutual enrichment.

MAKING YOUR OWN RUNES

You may wish to make your own Runes. Runes have been cut out of wood with the glyphs burned onto them. A particularly lovely set was created for me by a Navajo silversmith. Flat pebbles smoothed by the sea or a river make beautiful Runes. Runes can be made from quartz crystal, amethyst, jade, or pieces of bone.

The first set of Runes I commissioned was made of clay, twice glazed, by potter Norman Aufrichtig of Brookfield, Connecticut. While making the Viking Runes, he kept a daub of clay from each stone and then formed the Blank Rune from these daubs; thus the Blank Rune contained the symbolic clay of all life's elements.

If you make your own Runes, or make sets for others, let the doing be a meditation. The idea of meditating is a block for some people—including myself. I finally broke free from my anxiety about not being able to meditate conventionally when I heard mythologist Joseph Campbell say that underlining sentences in books was his meditation. Weeding in the garden can be a meditation. So can washing your car. Making your own Runes can be a profound and satisfying meditation.

LENDING YOUR RUNES

Finally, there remains the question of whether or not to lend your Runes to others. Some people will feel comfortable in lending them, others may not. Lending your Runes is a personal matter. When in doubt, simply ask by drawing a Rune from the bag: Upright means "Yes," Reversed means "No." If you happen to draw one of the Runes which reads the same Upright and Reversed, draw again.

Bridal song written in Runes, eleventh century

THE GREAT INVOCATION

From the point of Light within the mind of God
Let light stream forth into the minds of all.
Let Light descend on Earth.

From the point of Love within the Heart of God
Let Love stream forth into the hearts of all.
May Christ return to Earth.

From the center where the Will of God is known
Let purpose guide our little wills—
The purpose which the Masters know
and serve.

From the center which we call the human race
Let the Plan of Love and Light work out
And may it seal the door where evil
dwells.

Let Light and Love and Power
Restore the Plan on Earth.

—Alice Bailey

RUNEMAL: THE ART
OF RUNE CASTING

Remember, you cannot abandon what you do not know. To go beyond yourself, you must know yourself.

—Sri Nisargadatta Maharaj

Like many games, sacred and secular, the Runes are meant to be "played" upon a field. The field represents the world that is always coming to be and passing away. You may want to use a special piece of fabric, colored or white, that you keep for this purpose alone. When you unfold the cloth that serves as your field, that very act can become a silent meditation. My field, a rainbow weaving created by Patrick Shepherd, a weaver of the Findhorn Community in Scotland, measures 14 inches by 18 inches and is woven from twenty-two graded hues of silk thread.

My first bag was a found object: purple with a legend stitched on one side announcing that the bag's original contents had been a bottle of Crown Royal whiskey. Someone else drank the whiskey; I inherited the bag. There is something very satisfying about reaching into a bag and choosing the stones. I like feeling the stones click against one another and, even more, the way a Rune often seems to insert itself between my fingers.

But neither bag nor field needs to be ornate; as the *I Ching* reminds us, "Even with slender means, the sentiments of the heart can be expressed."

In ancient times, the Rune caster would chant an invocation to Odin, requesting that the god be present, and then scatter the stones onto the earth, taking counsel from those that fell glyph-side up. If this venerable method seems unwieldy to you, a number of other satisfactory techniques recommend themselves.

ODIN'S RUNE

This is the most practical and simple use of the Oracle and consists of selecting one Rune for an overview of an entire situation. Drawing a single Rune can help you to focus more clearly on your issue and provide you with a fresh perspective. What you are in effect doing is inviting the mind to function intuitively.

Odin's Rune is particularly helpful under stressful conditions. You may find yourself dealing with matters that demand action now, and the truth is *you don't have enough information.* To reach a decision, all you require is your bag of Runes and, if possible, a quiet place.

A friend who is a senior corporate officer recently

told me that he had suddenly been confronted with a crisis which amounted to taking over the company or resigning. "I headed for the men's room, clutching my bag of Runes," he said. "When I came out, I was on my way to becoming the Chief Executive Officer." The Rune he had drawn was *Dagaz* ⋈ , the Rune of break-through and transformation.

Drawing a single Rune is not only valuable in a time of crisis: The technique is useful any time you want an overview of your situation. On a long drive or commute between home and work, some people keep their Runes beside them on the seat. Drawing Odin's Rune often reveals the humor in a difficult matter. And why not? God's favorite music is said to be laughter.

If you are concerned about someone who is far away and you are unable to contact that person, focus directly on the individual, and then draw a Rune. This practice opens a doorway in the mind to the non-ordinary. You may find that it is, indeed, possible to know things at a distance.

Use the single Rune drawing to honor significant events in your life: birthdays, the New Year, solstices and equinoxes, the death of a friend, births, anniversaries, and other special occasions. You may want to record these castings in a Rune Journal (see page 60).

THREE RUNE SPREAD

The number "three" figures prominently in the divinatory practices of the ancients. The *Three Rune Spread*, which, according to Tacitus, was already in use 2,000 years ago, is satisfactory for all but the most extended and intricate readings.

With an issue clearly in mind, select three Runes, one at a time, and place them, in order of selection, from *right to left*. To avoid consciously changing the direction of the stones, especially as you become familiar with their symbols, you may want to place them blank side up, and then turn them over.

Once you have selected the Runes, they will lie before you in this fashion: Reading from the right, the first Rune speaks to the *Situation as It Is;* the second Rune (center) suggests the *Course of Action Called For;* and the third Rune (on the left) indicates the *New Situation That Will Evolve,* after you have successfully met your challenge.

New Situa-tion	Action	Situa-tion
3	2	1

How you happen to turn the stones may still alter the direction of the glyphs to either an Upright or Reversed position, but this, too, is part of the process. Since only nine Runes read the same Upright and Reversed, the readings for the other sixteen will depend on how you turn the stones.

A Sample Reading

A friend came to me for a Rune casting after his wife had left him. He was experiencing a great deal of pain, realizing how much the relationship meant to him and agonizing over his loss. His issue was, "What am I to learn from this separation?"

These are the Runes he drew:

The three Runes were interpreted in the following manner: Reading from the right, the first Rune, *Algiz* ⍵, the Rune of Protection Reversed, addresses his sense of being totally vulnerable, unprotected. It is a counsel to be mindful that only right action and correct conduct provide protection at such a time. He must learn and grow from this loss. The second Rune, *Kano* ⟨, is the Rune of Opening. He is encouraged to trust his process and consider what aspects of his old conditioning must change. Third came *Nauthiz* ⍦, the Rune of Constraint and Pain. The new growth will not be free of anguish. And yet his wife's departure may prompt him to undertake serious work on himself; he is reminded that rectification must come before progress.

To sum up, the three Runes are saying that, although he is feeling vulnerable and exposed, with the pain comes the necessary clarity to get on with the work of self-change. As he progresses, he is reminded to consider the positive uses of adversity.

FIVE RUNE SPREAD

Drawing a single Rune—Odin's Rune—will, as a rule, provide sufficient information to enable you to proceed with right action and skillful means. And yet, moments occur when the need-to-know extends beyond the authority of a single stone. Employing the *Five Rune Spread* breaks out the distinctive features of a situation that might overwhelm you with its complexity or uncertainty.

Begin by clearly formulating your issue. Then draw five stones from the bag, one at a time, and place them one below the other. In descending order, let the Runes stand for:

(1) Overview of the Situation
(2) Challenge
(3) Course of Action Called For
(4) Sacrifice
(5) Evolved Situation

If you select five Runes, and place them one below the other in front of you, the odds against drawing this particular spread are 607,614 to 1. If, however, you decide to mark down the Rune you select and then return it to the bag, you will be making each selection from a full set of Runes, and the odds against drawing this particular spread soar to 312,500,000 to 1. As you can see, the Five Rune Spread is highly personal and specific.

The term *Sacrifice,* in the fourth position, is intended as a recognition that life offers you choices, options, that are often mutually exclusive. The concept of sacrifice has, over time, come to be associated primarily with pain and loss. As used in the Five Rune Spread, however, the term sacrifice refers to that which has to be peeled away, shed, discarded (as is called for in the Rune *Othila*), in order for new wholeness to emerge. Originally a bonding of two Latin words *(sacrificium* and *facere),* one of the core meanings of sacrifice is "surrender to God."

A Sample Reading

Leila had created a successful business in partnership with her husband. Basically, the creative impulse, the idea and slogging hard work of getting the company on its feet, had been hers. In essence, the company was her "baby." Now it was time to take the baby public and the new investors wanted her ongoing participation, but not her husband's. All her fears regarding loyalty, abandonment, the risk to her marriage and her husband's self-esteem, were brought up by this

situation. So Leila decided to do the Five Rune Spread.
The following is what she drew:

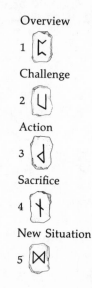

Overview

1

Challenge

2

Action

3

Sacrifice

4

New Situation

5

Drawing *Perth* ⸤ᛈ⸥ , the Rune of Initiation, as the
Overview of the situation, immediately shifted her focus
away from both her relationship with her husband and
the business. *Nothing external matters here, except as it shows
you its inner reflection*—these words were key for her. She
read the words over and over, then realized that this
was another crossroad in the process of self-change.

In the *Challenge* position came *Uruz Reversed,* ⸤ᚢ⸥ ,
the Rune of Strength and Womanhood, indicating the
need to respond consciously to "the demands of such

a creative time." It was clear to her that the correct decision was for growth at all levels, corporate as well as personal.

The *Course of Action Called For* brought *Wunjo Reversed* ᚹ, which speaks of the "process of birth" being long and arduous, and about fears which arise for the safety of "the child" within. Again, the Runes were reminding Leila that this was a test.

The Rune of *Sacrifice* was *Nauthiz Reversed* ᚾ, the Rune of Constraint, Necessity and Pain, the great teacher in the guise of pain and limitation. She was able to see more clearly that it was time to take a new kind of responsibility for what she had created, to own and honor it, and do what was good for the company.

Leila smiled with pleasure as she drew *Dagaz* ᛞ, Breakthrough, Transformation, for the *New Situation Evolving.* This Rune offers the assurance that "because the timing is right, the outcome is assured, although not, from the present vantage point, predictable."

Several months after Leila's company had gone public, her husband started a new business of his own in which his talents were soon to generate his own success.

THE RUNIC CROSS

This spread is useful when you want a more complete picture of any situation. Inspired by the Tarot, the layout calls for selecting six Runes, which are set out in the form of a Runic or Celtic Cross. The pattern is as follows:

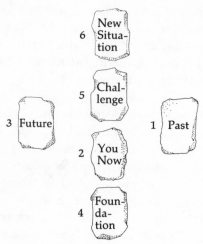

The first Rune represents the *Past,* that from which you are coming, what lies directly behind you. The second Rune represents *You Now.* The third, or *Future* Rune, stands for what lies ahead of you, what is coming into being. The fourth Rune gives the foundation of the matter under consideration, the unconscious elements and archetypal forces involved. The fifth, or *Challenge* Rune, indicates the nature of the obstacles in your path. The final Rune indicates the *New Situation* that will evolve as you successfully meet your challenge.

Since a considerable amount of information is contained in the Runic Cross, this spread often provides the incentive for deep thought and reflection. If, after laying out and considering these six Runes, you still lack clarity, replace all the Runes in their bag and draw a single Rune. This seventh Rune, *the Rune of Resolution*, will help you to recognize the essence of the situation.

THREE LIFETIMES SPREAD

This spread is for those who wish to experiment with the idea of reincarnation. It furnishes a three-level perspective on your passage, and is laid out in the form of the Rune of Fertility, *Inguz* ⟨�)(⟩ . The Runes represent (1) Birth and Childhood Conditions, (2) Your Present, (3) Future in this Life, (4) Past Incarnation and (5) Future Incarnation. The Runes are placed in the following manner:

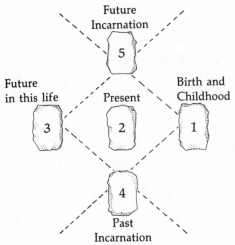

Future
Incarnation

5

Future
in this life

3

Present

2

Birth and
Childhood

1

4

Past
Incarnation

The Three Lifetimes Spread provides you with information concerning unresolved aspects of your past. Once these elements are recognized, you can change your present situation, thus affecting both your future in this life and your next soul cycle.

A Sample Reading

The first reading I undertook with the Three Lifetimes Spread was on my own account.

Birth and Childhood Conditions informs me that I came into this life to receive the gift of *Nauthiz* ⟨↑⟩ , the Rune of Constraint and Pain. Now I must learn to work with the undeveloped aspects of myself, areas of stunted growth, weaknesses I project onto others. I was put on notice that I could expect setbacks until I understood the source of my suffering.

My *Present* is signified by *Jera* ⟨◇⟩ , the Rune of Beneficial Outcomes, a span of time leading to Harvest, during which I am called to exercise patience and cultivate my nature with care.

My *Future in this Life* is represented by *Sowelu* ⟨ϟ⟩ ,

the Rune of Wholeness, Life Force, the impulse toward self-realization and regeneration, the recognition of something long denied and the attendant warning not to give myself airs.

Dagaz ⋈ , the Rune of Transformation, stands in the *Past Incarnation* position. It indicates that a major transformation comes through developing compassion for myself and others by addressing my own suffering and understanding its source.

Finally, the *Future Incarnation* is represented by *Eih-waz* ⌡ , the Rune of Avertive Powers and Defense. The only defense is skillful means, that is to say, the realization of the qualities of patience, perseverence and resoluteness. These are the skillful means which will open the door to new life.

RUNE PLAY

This game is not about winning or losing. *Rune Play* focuses on whatever issue people want to examine, and play continues until such time as that issue seems adequately clarified to all players. If possible, each player should have a set of Runes, although one set will suffice. If only one bag is used, however, the dynamics of the game are altered significantly.

Select three Runes from your bag and place them in front of you, glyph side down. The first player turns over a Rune and interprets it as it relates to the issue. Then, the next player turns over a Rune, gives an interpretation, and has the option of relating it to the previous Rune. The third player turns over a Rune, gives an interpretation, and has the option of commenting on the two previous Runes. When the round is completed, repeat the process for the second and third rounds. You may wish to play a final round in which each of the players, in turn, tells what new insights have come to them concerning the issue.

Rune Play can be enjoyed by a close-knit group of colleagues or associates working on a project. Say you are doing research and development on a new invention and the process is blocked. Three or four of you may want to declare a Rune Play break. A variation on the three Rune progression might prove useful in such a situation: *You Now* (first round), *Your Part in the Blockage* (second round) and *Remedy* (third round). The game swiftly takes on strategic and therapeutic overtones. Everyone will learn something, and there will be no lack of humor along the way.

For more intimate issues, two-handed Rune Play can be illuminating. Any two people can play this game when some issue calls for clarification. The number of Runes you choose is up to you. To keep friction at a minimum—if the situation is particularly sensitive—you may decide not to comment on one another's Runes until play is complete.

A Sample Game

A couple whose relationship was in trouble decided on a game of Rune Play. This is what followed:

She played *Laguz Reversed* ⎣⏉⎦ , the Rune of Water, Flow, That Which Conducts, interpreting it as a statement to her husband to get in touch with his intuitive self if he hopes to understand her. He played *Raido,* ⎡R⎤ , the Rune of Journey, Communication, Union and Reunion, which he saw as evidence of his willingness to keep on removing resistances, regulating excesses. On the second round, she played *Hagalaz* ⎡N⎤ , the Rune of Disruptive Natural Forces, Elemental Power, indicating an urge for freedom, a warning that she will, if necessary, sacrifice security and relationship in order to grow. He played *Uruz* ⎡∩⎤ , the Rune of Strength, Manhood, an indication that he, too, is going through a transition— reclaiming part of himself, a part he has been living out through another. As they continued to play, they became conscious of the fact that they were both in a period of accelerated self-change and needed to make an effort to hear each other more clearly.

Watching a hand develop can be most revealing although not, on every occasion, free of discomfort. But then, true growth rarely is.

THE CYCLE OF INITIATION

Thirteen of the twenty-five Runes focus directly on the mechanism of self-change. You may find it useful to watch for the Thirteen as you undergo your passage since, taken together, they comprise a *Cycle of Initiation.* These Runes make up an energy framework

58

within the body of the runic alphabet; an armature, so to speak, facilitating and sustaining the process of self-change.

The Thirteen are: (3) *Ansuz,* Signals, the Messenger Rune; (4) *Othila,* Separation, Retreat, Inheritance; (5) *Uruz,* Strength, Manhood/Womanhood; (6) *Perth,* Initiation, Something Hidden; (7) *Nauthiz,* Constraint, Necessity, Pain; (8) *Inguz,* Fertility, New Beginnings; (14) *Kano,* Opening, Fire; (16) *Berkana,* Growth, Rebirth; (17) *Ehwaz,* Movement, Progress; (19) *Hagalaz,* Disruptive Natural Forces, Elemental Power; (20) *Raido,* Communication, Union, Reunion; (21) *Thurisaz,* Gateway, Place of Non-Action; (22) *Dagaz,* Breakthrough, Transformation.

Whenever two or more of the Thirteen Cycle Runes are conjoint in a spread, the potential for growth and integration is greatly enhanced.

Technique

Isolate the thirteen Runes in their bag. Settle yourself quietly, aware that, rather than posing an issue for the Runes to comment upon, you are asking your unconscious for direction, petitioning the Higher Self to advise you: What requires special attention? What aspect of your Nature, if cared for, modified, understood, nurtured, will carry you forward in the journey of the self toward the Self?

Now draw a Rune to learn where you are in the Cycle of Initiation. See if the Runes' sense of your position accords with your own.

Sample Reading

Fehu ⟨ᛉ⟩ , Signals, the Messenger Rune, is telling you that this is the moment of new life unfolding. You are at the beginning of a new Cycle. It is time to make conscious what is unconscious, particularly an awareness that self-nourishment is both possible and timely. You are asked to allow the Self to nourish the self, for it is only then that you will truly be in a position to nourish others.

Next draw a Rune from all twenty-five stones in order to know how you are to proceed, and what requires attention in order to recognize the Signals that are timely to your Nature.

The Rune drawn is *Thurisaz* ⟨ᚦ⟩ , the Gateway, another of the Cycle Runes. It recommends contemplating your progress to date, the quality of your path, and the encounters that are taking place on that path. You may, if you wish, pick yet another Rune to ask for more clarity.

As you grow in clarity, others will see it, and new opportunities will be afforded you. From the self to the Self the word goes out; from the Self to the Divine. Then, according to your preparation, the answer comes. As Mother Teresa has said, "God loves the world through us." By heeding the call of the Cycle of Initiation, you are indeed opening yourself to the message of the Divine in your life.

KEEPING A RUNE JOURNAL

As you establish your practice of working with the Runes, you may find it helpful to record the guidance you receive. You may want to mark down the particular stones cast and a brief interpretation in your journal.* Note the time, date, and the prevailing conditions in your life at the moment. Keeping such a journal allows you to observe the quality of your progress as you work with the Runes.

A technique that Dr. Allan W. Anderson suggests to students of the *I Ching* is equally valid for those who work with the Runes. He calls it "The Rule of Right Action." Each morning consult the Oracle to determine your Rule of Right Action for the day. Draw one Rune, record it in your journal, and let it serve as your guidance for the day. Sometimes, when it has been a particularly trying or exhilarating day, you may wish to consult the Oracle again in the evening for an evaluation of how you've conducted yourself. If the idea of asking for a daily Rule seems excessive, try it on a weekly basis. Consult the Runes on Monday for the week's Rule of Right Action, then draw another Rune on Sunday night for your evaluation.

Recording these readings in your Rune Journal will help you to become more familiar with the Runes and their symbolism and, over time, will enable you to

---

*Rune Play, A Seasonal Record Book with Twelve New Techniques for Rune Casting, by Ralph Blum, was published by St. Martin's Press in 1985.

judge for yourself the relevance and accuracy of the Oracle as a guide to self-change.

As you become familiar with the Runes, you will no doubt discover new and creative ways to utilize them. The Viking Runes, ancient as they are, remain an open-ended system. Enjoy your Runes, play with them, let them speak to you. We at the RuneWorks would appreciate hearing from you about your own experiences with the Oracle.

A SIMPLE PRAYER

Lord, make me an instrument of your peace.
Where there is hatred, let me sow love.
Where there is injury, let me sow pardon.
Where there is doubt, let me sow faith.
Where there is despair, let me sow hope.
Where there is darkness, let me sow light.
Where there is sadness, let me sow joy.
O Divine Master, grant that
I may not so much seek
To be consoled as to console,
To be understood as to understand,
To be loved as to love.
For it is in giving that we receive.
It is in pardoning that we are pardoned.
It is in dying that we are born to eternal life.

—St. Francis of Assisi

Eighth century; whale bone.

RUNECRAFT:
THREE NEW SPREADS

In our contemporary world of instant everything, these exercises call us to remember the cyclical nature of life, the processional quality of personal growth. Whether it takes the form of cleansing, setting things right in a relationship, or the completion of one of life's cycles, taking the time to acknowledge and make conscious what you are about to do will invariably enrich your experience.

The three exercises which follow are intended to serve in the reintroduction of ritual into our daily lives.

WATER RUNES

This exercise is linked to the Rune *Laguz* ⎡⎤ , whose attributes are "water, fluidity, the ebb and flow of emotions, of vocations and relationships." This Rune casting can be performed whenever your body comes in contact with water. It is a cleansing, healing ritual.

Any time you dip your hands into water or take a shower or jump into a pool, a lake, the ocean, think or speak these words:

I cleanse myself of all selfishness,
Resentment,
Critical emotions toward my fellow beings,
Self-condemnation,
And ignorant misinterpretations of my life's experiences.

Watch what comes to mind as you repeat these words aloud or in silence. Use this Prayer of Intention with love and gentleness, for it is not a hair shirt you are putting on; you are not making yourself wrong. Rather, you are embodying in words a yearning for more clarity, more Light in your life.

Then again, you may prefer to transform the selfishness, resentment, and self-condemnation into their *light opposites,* repeating the Prayer of Intention in the following form:

I bathe myself in generosity,
Appreciation,
Emotions of praise toward my fellow beings,
Self-acceptance,
And enlightened understanding of my life's experiences.

Select a Rune on the issue of Self-condemnation and Self-acceptance on one day. On another day you might draw a Rune relating to Selfishness and Generosity. You may wish to draw a Rune concerning a particular life experience that has become fixed in memory as distasteful, shameful or embarrassing, asking for new Light by which to grow in understanding of the truth and appropriateness of that life experience.

The occasions for using the *Water Runes* are limitless. There is no activity that is less sacred than any other. Washing the dishes, the dog, or the pickup will do nicely, as will bathing the baby, watering the lawn, or standing in the rain.

You may wish to write out this Prayer of Intention and tape it to the shower wall, the splashboard over your sink, the water cooler. When the words run and dissolve, write them out and stick them up again. Let the Water Runes Ceremony flow with your life.

RUNES OF RECTIFICATION

rectify 1. to put or set right; correct; amend; 2. to adjust, as in movement or balance . . .
        —*Webster's New World Dictionary of the American Language*

This is a technique for those times when problems arise between co-workers, friends, lovers, and others who collaborate across boundaries of understanding and temperament.

When something occurs that causes dissension or blockage, come together with the intention of bringing Light to the situation. Here the procedure is reversed from the usual, in that the Rune casting comes at the end of the process. The core of the process is the asking and answering of five questions:

(1) What happened?
(2) How do you feel about what happened?
(3) How would you do it differently next time?
(4) What results would you like to see?
(5) What insight have you gained from what happened?

Close the door and unplug the telephone. Be sure to allow enough time for a) all participants to answer each question, b) for discussion and, c) for the drawing of Runes to further clarify the issue.

One person may elect to take notes while the others speak. Each question should be addressed by all of the participants before proceeding to the next question. Cross-talk or responding to someone while they are speaking is to be discouraged. Statements of *how you feel* (hurt, angry, self-conscious, afraid) rather than statements of "what you did to me" or "what you did wrong," will help to keep the question period from dissolving into self-justification or acrimony. During this process, agree to suspend judgment for the sake of better understanding. Keep it light. Keep it clear.

Finally, after everyone has had the opportunity to express their feelings regarding each question, encourage any of the participants who still require clarification on a particular issue to pick a Rune. One of you might be disturbed or confused about feelings you expressed in answer to question #2, *How do you feel about what happened?* Perhaps there is disagreement among the participants as to what really took place. If so, an overview of the key events can be provided by selecting a Rune for question #1, *What happened?* It will be up to each of you to address the questions about which you are still dissatisfied or unclear.

When all is said and done, one of the group may wish to draw a final Rune to comment on the essence of the matter in the Light of the process of rectification.

RUNES OF COMFORT FOR THE BEREAVED

If you have unfinished business with someone who has died, simply take a moment to visualize the person you want to remember. Use a favorite photograph if you have one. Then make a list of the matters you would have liked to discuss, the things you wish you had shared but didn't. Draw a Rune on each issue and meditate on the response. Letters received from people who have worked with the Runes in this way indicate that the results are invariably heartening.

A young man whose mother had recently been killed in an automobile accident wanted to know what she would have advised him before she died. He drew *Teiwaz* ⇑ , Warrior Energy. "Be a Spiritual Warrior—that's exactly what she would have said!"

"When my grief was choking me," wrote a Florida woman about the death of her twin sister, "I picked a Rune on the issue 'What would Clara be saying to me now?' and got *Inguz* ⧈ , Fertility and New Beginnings.

I began to laugh and laugh for I had just kept my promise to spread her ashes on the roses."

This process is not to be confused with séances or night letters from beyond the veil. Perhaps what the Runes do here is access your deep knowing about the person, knowing which is lodged in your own sub-conscious. When we hear the voice of Truth, we recognize it.

The prayer that follows is the result of a meditation on one such Rune casting when *Dagaz* ⋈ , the Rune of Breakthrough and Transformation, was drawn.

RUNES OF COMFORT
FOR THE BEREAVED

I am the Life and the Light and the Way—
The earth is my Garden.
Each of the Souls I plant as seeds
Germinates and flowers in its season,
And in each I am fulfilled.
There is no cause for grief
When a blossom fades
But only rejoicing for the beauty it held
And praise that my Will is done
And my Plan served.
I am one with all creatures
And none is ever lost
But only restored to me,
Having never left me at all.
For what is Eternal
Cannot be separated from its Source.
I am with you all,
And each of you is a channel for my Light.
Feel my Love
Enfold you now and evermore.

6

A DESTINY
PROFILE

In undertaking the work of self-change, we are asked to examine the foundations of our lives. We hear it said in many camps, by spiritual teachers of all persuasions, that we are to "discover the teacher within." What we need now are some useful techniques for listening to ourselves.

One such technique was devised by Dr. Allan W. Anderson for use with the *I Ching,* the Chinese Book of Changes. He calls it *A Destiny Profile.* The Profile, which consists of six questions, comprises a grid within which a human life can be framed.

The Destiny Profile adapts itself well to use with the Viking Runes. However, there is a seriousness about this spread that sets the Destiny Profile apart from other Runic exercises. According to Dr. Anderson, the six questions that make up the Profile shall be asked *only once* in the course of one's lifetime. This restriction may at first seem daunting, especially in our "try, try again" culture. We don't like limitation. And yet, the gift the Destiny Profile conveys is the *creative essence of limitation.*

Asked "What are we to be made conscious of through the Destiny Profile?" the Runes replied with *Laguz* $\boxed{\mathsf{l}}$, the Rune of Water, Flow, That Which Conducts, *Reversed:*

> A warning against overreach, excessive striving, a counsel against trying to exceed your own strength or operate beyond the power you have funded to date in your life.

This is a reading that focuses on the nature of limitation.

You may wish to defer drawing the Runes for the Destiny Profile until you have considered the idea for a while. Long thoughts about the way you have lived your life until now may be appropriate before you proceed. When you are ready to begin, perhaps you will want to ask the first question, receive the Oracle's commentary, then consider that commentary for a time before proceeding to the second question. Or you may elect to ask all six questions at one sitting, but study them one at a time over an extended period. Let the receptive side of your Warrior Nature be your guide.

After drawing your Rune for the first question, record it, then replace the Rune in the bag. Each question must be posed with a complete set of Runes. When recording the Runes that you draw, place them in a vertical line, with the first Rune at the top, and then write down your thoughts about the Oracle's response. You may wish to review your

Destiny Profile from time to time, adding new insights as they occur to you.

Here, then, are the six questions that comprise the Destiny Profile, each followed by a sample reading.

(1) WHAT IS MY NATURE?

In asking the question "What is my Nature?" you are concerning yourself with the material cause of your Nature, what you were born with. For your Nature is a constellation of possibilities, *and* it is surrounded and circumscribed by numerous impossibilities.

Begin by examining your limitations: You come from a certain background, you have lived your life in a particular way, you have a heart condition, you can't have children—whatever the case may be. As your limitations become clearer to you, you will begin to see that various notions you hold about yourself are *not* supported by the reality of your life. And yet, as your Nature is limited by what you cannot do or be, it is also *specified* by what you can. Through this process of limiting and specifying, your view of yourself will become clearer and more simple. As you simplify, you find the power to work with your Nature, with the substance out of which your Destiny is to be realized.

A Sample Reading

Ehwaz $\bowtie$, the Rune of Movement, Progress, *Reversed.* "Movement that appears to block" speaks to your inability to recognize what is timely to your Nature and what is not. First, work on yourself to strengthen your interior life; when that is strong enough, what needs to be accomplished will become apparent to you. The feeling that you are missing out will be replaced by the desire to avoid action until it is timely. But if you insist on forging ahead unstrengthened, your Nature will turn against everything you do that is premature, for Destiny cannot be humbugged, wheedled, or influenced. There is an old saying that "What is for you will not pass by you." Or, as *Ehwaz* expresses it, "As I cultivate my own nature, all else follows."

(2) WHY WAS I BORN?

The meaning of the question is this: "What is the lack or privation with which I have come into the world, whose satisfaction will empower my continuing growth in keeping with the Will of the Divine?" In other words, *What is Heaven's mandate for me?* In addressing this question, you are preparing to discover what is missing in your makeup that you are here to acquire— patience, courage in the face of adversity, or any other underdeveloped aspect of your self, the acquiring of which will enable you to navigate your ideal passage through this life.

A Sample Reading

Sowelu $\boxed{\varsigma}$, the Rune of Wholeness, stands for "that which your Nature requires. It embodies the impulse toward self-realization and indicates the path you must follow, not from ulterior motives but from the core of your individuality." It is said that the mark of the Spiritual Warrior is impeccability. Living impeccably means to strive at all times to do what is appropriate. To this end, you are "required to face and vanquish your refusal to let right action flow through you."

Your quest as a Spiritual Warrior is to seek after Wholeness in the sense of bringing together that which requires unification. This Rune focuses on the ability to "retreat in strength." In timely retreat, allow the Light into any part of you which has been kept in darkness. That darkness—the result of your privation—is the divided self, and timely right action will lead you to self-acceptance, self-healing, and Wholeness.

(3) WHAT IS MY VOCATION?

Vocation, as used here, does not mean what you do for a living. Drawing a Rune for Vocation will tell you how you are called to go through this life and what principles you must embody in your passage. If you conduct yourself properly according to Vocation, you will satisfy the privation, the lack, described in the answer to the question *"Why was I born?"* Through learning to relate correctly to severe privation you grow in the Spirit. That is why St. Paul says in Romans 4, "We rejoice in tribulations," since tribulations provide the occasions to meet privation courageously. In the process, you will increase in willpower and self-awareness. The principal goal of Vocation is to come to one's Self.

Sample Reading

Ewwaz ⟦M⟧ , Movement, Progress, specifies that your Vocation calls for "movement in the sense of improving or bettering any situation." Note that this Rune was also drawn Reversed in answer to the question *"What is my Nature?"* Drawing *Ewwaz* twice in the Profile emphasizes the idea of timely movement as crucial to the exercising of skillful means. Simply expressed, the principle is this: no acting needy, no lusting after outcomes.

Learn how to wait. Learn how to ask. Learn how to go solitary through the world. Then your Vocation ⟦M⟧ , will agree with your Nature ⟦W⟧ , and all movement will be in accord with the Will of Heaven.

There is an exercise, practiced by the Reverend Harry Haines, that seems relevant to the work required of you. Whenever he is called upon to deal with an issue where clarity is lacking, he does four things: "First I consider my own needs. Then I consider the needs of others. Next I consult with a wiser friend. And finally, I wait for the peace that passes understanding. Only then do I act."

(4) WHAT IS MY DESTINY?

Destiny, as used here, means *your ideal passage through this life, your ideal possibility*. There is no such thing as a "bad destiny," for your Destiny is the Divine's desire for your Highest Good. Your Destiny is your spiritual destination. There is an energy that ceaselessly moves us to change for good rather than ill, and that energy is the outworking of Divine Will in our lives.

At the same time, Destiny is confinement. Destiny is realized as the direct result of life's limitations. According to *Ehwaz*, "There are no missed opportunities: you have simply to recognize that not all opportunities are for you, that not all possibilities are open to you." If your limitations define what you may not do in the world, they also challenge you to accept yourself and get on with what it is you can do.

A Sample Reading

Perth [ᛈ] , the Rune of Initiation, *Reversed*. In drawing *Perth Reversed*, you are reminded that "Nothing external matters here, except as it shows you its inner reflection." *Perth* has associations with the Phoenix, "the mystical bird that consumes itself in the fire and then rises from its own ashes." Again and again, the Oracle is saying, you will go through the flames. Treat each obstruction in your path as a challenge specific to the initiation you are presently undergoing. Living your life as Initiation and responding well to the Will of Heaven is your Destiny.

(5) WHAT IS MY CROSS?

The Cross stands for a condition that lasts a life-time; it is your "ordeal" from birth to death. The answer to this question reveals the pattern of adversity you must undergo in order to increase in self-awareness and self-rule. Take up your cross voluntarily. For in so doing you are declaring your willingness to undergo the pattern of adversity ordained for you by the Will of Heaven. As you grow in awareness, you will come to recognize that certain features of adversity are yours to work with throughout your life. Many opportunities will be afforded you to meet the challenges represented by your Cross.

The Cross is the condition for wisdom. Christ on the Tree. Odin on the Tree. Each of us on the Tree. The Cross stands for that without which there can be no getting of wisdom.

A Sample Reading

Eihwaz ⟨↕⟩ , Avertive Powers, Defense. "As we are tested we fund the power to avert blockage and defeat," this Rune is saying. "At the same time, we develop in ourselves an aversion to the conduct that creates stress in our lives." Learn to regard delays and blockages as potentially beneficial, to see that, through inconvenience and discomfort, growth is promoted.

There is a tendency in your Nature to surpass the limits proper to that Nature. This tendency—to push beyond where good can be achieved—calls for a Cross, a pattern of adversity, of being thwarted each time your actions are inappropriate. All that is asked of you is to go through the world well.

(6) WHAT IS MY UNIFIED SELF?

In seeking the image of your Unified Self, ask for the qualities that will emerge in your life when your intellect and will begin to work in harmony with your physical being and feelings. To act uncontrivedly and in a timely manner are the signs that one is in accord with one's Unified Self. Seek to discover the teacher within, for then you have a reliable source for understanding the component forces you must work with in order to achieve your Unified Self.

A Sample Reading

Uruz ⋂ , Strength, Manhood, Womanhood. The image of the Unified Self will emerge as the old bonds are severed, when that which has outgrown its form can die, releasing its energy in a new birth, a new form. The Rune of "termination and new beginnings," *Uruz* exemplifies a willingness on your part to embrace change and to recognize that, in the life of the Spirit, you are always at the beginning.

In ancient times, *Uruz* was symbolized by the aurochs, the wild ox, a difficult animal to domesticate. Drawing this Rune in response to the question *"What is my Unified Self?"* indicates that to achieve self-unification, you must undertake to harness and gentle the wild creature within by becoming one with it through your compassionate understanding of its nature and needs. Develop your will by setting a firm intention, by visualizing the form your Unified Self will take. With time, that form will expand; as you embrace the image of the expanded form, that image will continue to evolve and self-understanding will increase.

A beginning has been made. Once the elements of your Destiny Profile have been identified, you will begin to see how they fit together. Through focusing on the correlation between "What is my Vocation?" (the occasion for acquiring strength) and "Why was I Born?" (the privation you came into the world with), you can begin to relate correctly to undeveloped and disowned aspects of yourself. As your knowledge of your self increases, so will your self-acceptance, and you will experience the meaning and joy of living your life in a *true present.* It is through letting go of your attachments to the past and your expectations for the future that you will experience a *true present,* which is the only time in which self-change can be realized.

The Destiny Profile is a tool to be used as you persevere in the finest art of all, the art of self-change. Remember: Self-change is never coerced; we are always free to resist. And if there is one thing to bear in mind until the truth of its words eases the heart troubled by apparent failure and loss, it is this: *The new life is always greater than the old.*

Finally, as you change and grow, your understanding of the six readings in your Destiny Profile will also change and grow—grow, perhaps, to include an appreciation that asking the questions only once was enough.

Picture stone at När Smiss, Gotland, Sweden.

A WARRIOR'S CREED

I have no parents: I make the heavens and earth my parents.

I have no home: I make awareness my home.

I have no life or death: I make the tides of breathing my life and death.

I have no divine power: I make honesty my divine power.

I have no means: I make understanding my means.

I have no magic secrets: I make character my magic secret.

I have no body: I make endurance my body.

I have no eyes: I make the flash of lightning my eyes.

I have no ears: I make sensibility my ears.

I have no limbs: I make promptness my limbs.

I have no strategy: I make "unshadowed by thought" my strategy.

I have no designs: I make "seizing opportunity by the forelock" my design.

I have no miracles: I make right-action my miracles.

I have no principles: I make adaptability to all circumstances my principles.

I have no tactics: I make emptiness and fullness my tactics.

I have no talents: I make ready wit my talent.

I have no friends: I make my mind my friend.

I have no enemy: I make carelessness my enemy.

I have no armor: I make benevolence and righteousness my armor.

I have no castle: I make immovable-mind my castle.

I have no sword: I make absence of self my sword.

—Anonymous Samurai, fourteenth century

7

INTERPRETING
THE RUNES

The final part of this book is the only part you really need—that and your set of Rune stones. In approaching an ancient mystery a surrender is required. As the Sufi poet Rumi wrote: *Let the beauty we love be what we do. / There are hundreds of ways to kneel and kiss the ground.*

Imagine a vast misty field containing some Stonehenge that did not survive. It lies within view of a glacier, this field, high above the mouth of a wild fjord. Out of the mists emerge massive, weathered stones, blossoming with yellow lichen. Above the rustle of feather grass, the deeply carved glyph in the center of each stone seems to pulse and vibrate. At the very center, touched by the sun's first rays, stands a blank and solitary stone: *both pregnant and empty, arbiter of all that is coming to be and passing away . . .*

These stones are the markers left by Spiritual Warriors, the servants of civilization. The praying voices of the Old Ones are silent. Hundreds of years have passed. No doubt those voices have whispered to others as they now whisper to us. It remains for us to honor our own natures and know the Stillness Within.

To that end, a single question, a simple prayer, will always suffice: *Show me what I need to know for my life now.*

Two daughters commissioned this stone in memory of their father. A work by the famous carver, Balle. Vårfrukyrka, Uppland, Sweden.

RUNE
INTERPRETATIONS

The Self

The starting point is the self. Its essence is water. Only clarity, willingness to change, is effective now. A correct relationship to your self is primary, for from it flow all possible correct relationships with others and with the Divine.

Remain modest—that is the Oracle's counsel. Regardless of how great may be your merit, be yielding, devoted and moderate, for then you have a true direction for your way of life.

Be in the world but not of it, that is implicit here. And yet do not be closed, narrow, or judging, but remain receptive to impulses flowing from the Divine within and without. *Strive to live the ordinary life in a non-ordinary way.* Remember at all times what is coming to be and passing away, and focus on that which abides. Nothing less is called for from you now.

This is a time of major growth and rectification and, as a rule, rectification must come before progress. The field is tilled before the seed is planted, the garden is weeded before the flower blooms, and the self must know stillness before it can discover its true song.

This is not a time to seek credit for accomplishments or to focus on results. Rather, be content to do your task for the task's sake. This is more a problem for those whose eyes are always on the goal than for those who have not forgotten how to play and can more easily find themselves in doing the work for its own sake. Herein lies the secret of experiencing a *true present.*

If you take the Rune of the Self and cut it down the middle, you will see the Rune for Joy with its mirror image. There is a subtle caution here against carelessness. The dancing acrobatic energy of balancing is called for now—the Self is required to balance the self. *Nothing in excess* was the second phrase written over the gateway to the temple at Delphi. The first counsel was *Know thyself.*

Reversed: If you feel blocked, do not turn to others, but look inside, in silence, for the enemy of your progress. No matter what area of your life seems to be impeded, stop and consider: You will recognize the outer "enemy" as but a reflection of what you have not, until now, been able or willing to recognize as coming from within.

Above all do not give yourself airs. Breaking the momentum of past habits is the challenge here: In the life of the Spirit you are always at the beginning.

Partnership
A Gift

Drawing this Rune is an indication that Partnership in some form is at hand. But you are put on notice not to collapse yourself into that union. For true Partnership is only achieved by separate and whole beings who retain their uniqueness even as they unite. Remember to let the winds of Heaven dance between you.

There is another realm of Partnership that we are being called to consider. For the path of Partnership can lead you to the realization of a still greater union— union with the Higher Self, union with the Divine. The ultimate gift of this Rune is the realization of the Divine in all things: God always enters into equal partnerships.

Gebo, the Rune of Partnership, has no Reverse: It signifies the gift of freedom from which flow all other gifts.

3

Ansuz

Signals
Messenger Rune
The God Loki

The keynote here is receiving: messages, signals, gifts. Even a timely warning may be seen as a gift. When the Messenger Rune brings sacred knowledge, one is truly blessed, for the message may be that of a new life unfolding. New lives begin with new connections, surprising linkages that direct us onto new pathways. Take pains now to be especially aware during meetings, visits, chance encounters, particularly with persons wiser than yourself.

Loki is the ancient trickster from the pantheon of the Norse gods. He is the *heyeohkah* of the North American Indian, "a mocking shadow of the creator god," the bringer of benefits to humankind. Even scoundrels and arch-thieves can be bearers of wisdom. When you draw this Rune, expect the unexpected: The message is always a call, a call to new life.

Ansuz is the first of the thirteen Runes that make up the Cycle of Initiation—Runes that focus directly upon the mechanism of self-change—and as such, addresses your need to integrate unconscious motive with conscious intent. Drawing it tells you that connection with the Divine is at hand. For *Ansuz* is a signal to explore the depths, the foundations of life, and to experience the inexhaustible wellspring of the Divine in your nature.

At the same time, you are reminded that you must first draw from the well to nourish and give to yourself. Then there will be more than enough to nourish others. A new sense of family solidarity invests *Ansuz*.

Reversed: You may well be concerned over what appears to be failed communication, lack of clarity or awareness either in your past history or in a present situation. You may feel inhibited from accepting what is offered. A sense of futility, of wasted motion may overwhelm you. Remember, however, that what is happening is timely in your process. If the well is clogged, this is the moment for cleaning out the old. *Ansuz Reversed,* is saying: *Consider the uses of adversity.*

4

Othila

Separation

Retreat

Inheritance

Now is a time of separating paths. Old skins must be shed, outmoded relationships discarded. When this Rune appears in a spread, a peeling away is called for. Included in the Cycle of Initiation, *Othila* is a Rune of radical severance.

The proper action here is submission and, quite probably, retreat—knowing how and when to retreat and possessing the firmness of will to carry it out.

Real property is associated with *Othila,* for it is the Rune of acquisition and benefits. However, the benefits you receive, the "inheritance," may be derived from something you must give up. Such a surrender can be particularly difficult when that which you are called upon to give up or abandon is an aspect of your behavior, or some part of your cultural inheritance. For then you must look closely at what, until now, you have proudly claimed as your birthright. Whether it is your attachment to your position in society, to the work you do or even to your beliefs about your own nature, the separation called for now will free you to become more truly who you are.

⟨ ◊ ⟩ **Reversed:** This is not a time to be bound by old conditioning, old authority. Consider not only what will benefit you but what will benefit others, and act according to the Light you possess now in your life. Because you may be called upon to undertake a radical departure from old ways, total honesty is required. Otherwise, through negligence or refusal to see clearly, you may cause pain to others and damage to yourself.

Adaptability and skillful means are the methods to cultivate at this time. Yet you must wait for the universe to act. Upon receiving this Rune, remember: We do without doing and everything gets done.

5
Uruz

Strength
Manhood, Womanhood
A Wild Ox

The Rune of termination and new beginnings, drawing *Uruz* indicates that the life you have been living has outgrown its form. That form must die so that life energy can be released in a new birth, a new form. This is a Rune of passage and, as such, part of the Cycle of Initiation.

Growth and change, however, may involve passage into darkness as part of the cycle of perpetual renewal. As in Nature, the progression consists of five parts: death, decay, fertilization, gestation, rebirth. Events occurring now may well prompt you to undergo a death within yourself. Since self-change is never coerced—we are always free to resist—remain mindful that the new form, the new life, is always greater than the old.

Prepare, then, for opportunity disguised as loss. It could involve the loss of someone or something to which there is an intense emotional bond, and *through* which you are living a part of your life, a part that must now be retrieved so you can live it out for yourself. In

94

some way, that bond is being severed, a relationship radically changed, a death experienced. Seek among the ashes and discover a new perspective and new strength.

The original symbol for *Uruz* was the aurochs, a wild ox. When the wild ox was domesticated—a nearly impossible task—it could transport heavy loads. Learn to adapt yourself to the demands of such a creative time. Firm principles attach to this Rune, and at the same time humility is called for, since in order to rule you must learn how to serve. This Rune puts you on notice that your soul and the universe support the new growth.

Reversed: Without ears to hear and eyes to see, you may fail to take advantage of the moment. The result could well be an opportunity missed or the weakening of your position. It may seem that your own strength is being used against you.

For some, *Uruz Reversed* will serve to alert, providing clues in the form of minor failures and disappointments. For others, those more deeply unconscious or unaware, it may provide a hard jolt. Reversed, this Rune calls for some serious thoughts about the quality of your relationship to your Self.

But take heart. Consider the constant cycling of death and rebirth, the endless going and return. Everything we experience has a beginning, a middle, an end, and is followed by a new beginning. Therefore do not draw back from the passage into darkness. When in deep water, become a diver.

6

Perth

Initiation

Something Hidden

A Secret Matter

A hieratic or mystery Rune pointing to that which is beyond our frail manipulative powers. This Rune is on the side of Heaven, the Unknowable, and has associations with the phoenix, that mystical bird which consumes itself in the fire and then rises from its own ashes. Its ways are secret and hidden.

Powerful forces of change are at work here. Yet what is achieved is not easily or readily shared. After all, becoming whole, the means of it, is a profound secret.

On the side of the earthly or mundane, there may well be surprises; unexpected gains are not unlikely. On the side of human nature, this Rune is symbolized by the flight of the eagle. Soaring flight, free from entanglement, lifting yourself above the endless ebb and flow of ordinary life to acquire broader vision—all this is indicated here. This is the Rune of questing.

Another of the Cycle Runes, *Perth* stands at the heart of Initiation. *Nothing external matters here, except as it shows you its inner reflection.* This Rune is concerned with the deepest stratum of being, with the bedrock on which your destiny is founded. For some, *Perth* means experiencing a psychic death. If need be, let go of everything, no exceptions, no exclusions. Nothing less than renewal of the Spirit is at stake.

Reversed: A counsel against expecting too much, or expecting in the ordinary way, for the old way has come to an end: You simply cannot repeat the old and not suffer. Call in your scattered energies, concentrate on your own life at this moment, your own requirements for growth. More important, *Perth* counsels you not to focus on outcomes, nor to bind yourself with the memory of past achievements; in so doing, you rob yourself of a *true present,* which is the only time in which self-change can be realized.

You may feel overwhelmed with exhaustion from meeting obstruction upon obstruction in your passage. Yet you always have a choice: You can see all this apparent negativity as "bad luck," or you can recognize it as an obstacle course, a challenge specific to the Initiation you are presently undergoing. Then each setback, each humiliation, becomes a test of character. When your inner being is shifting and reforming on a deep level, patience, constancy and perseverance are called for. So stay centered, see the humor, and keep on keeping on.

7

Nauthiz

Constraint

Necessity

Pain

The necessity of dealing with severe Constraint is the lesson of *Nauthiz*. The positive aspects of this Rune represent the limitations we directly cause outselves; its negative side attracts limitations from those around us. Both are equally difficult to handle.

The role of *Nauthiz* is to identify our "shadow," our dark and repressed side, places where growth has been stunted, resulting in weaknesses that we project onto others. Don't take this world personally, this Rune is saying: Work with the shadow, examine what inside you magnetizes misfortune into your life. When at last you can look upon *Nauthiz* with a smile, you will recognize the troubles, denials, and setbacks of life as your teachers, guides and allies.

The need for restraint is unquestionable here. Drawing this Rune indicates that there will be holdups, reasons to reconsider your plans carefully. There is work to be done on your self. So take it on with good will and show perseverence.

This is a time to pay off old debts, to restore, if not

harmony, at least balance. So mend, restore, redress—when fishermen can't go to sea they repair nets. Let the Constraints of the time serve you in righting your relationship to your Self. Be mindful that rectification comes before progress. And once again, consider the uses of adversity.

Reversed: As part of the Cycle of Initiation, *Nauthiz* is the great teacher disguised as the bringer of pain and limitation. It has been said that only at the point of greatest darkness do we become aware of the Light within us by which we come to recognize the true creative power of the self.

When something within us is disowned, that which is disowned wreaks havoc. A cleansing is required here; in undertaking it you fund a will and strengthen character. Begin with what is most difficult and proceed to what is easy. Or, conversely, begin with what is easy and proceed to what is most difficult. Either way, remember that "suffering," in its original sense, merely meant "undergoing." Thus you are required to undergo the dark side of your passage, and bring it into the Light. Controlling your anger, restraining your impulses, keeping your faith firm—all this is at issue here. Modesty and good temper are essential at such a time.

8
Inguz

Fertility
New Beginnings
Ing, the Hero-God

This Rune is akin to the moon, the intuitive part of our nature, with its urge toward harmonizing and adjusting in the sphere of personal relationships. *Inguz* embodies the need to share, the yearning to be desired, a search after similarities.

The completion of beginnings is what *Inguz* requires. It may mark a time of joyous deliverance, of new life, a new path. A Rune of great power, drawing it means that you now have the strength to achieve completion, resolution, from which comes a new beginning. Above all, completion is crucial here. It may be timely that you complete some project now; if so, make that your first priority. Perhaps a difficult state of mind can be resolved, clarified, turned around. Drawing this Rune indicates that you must fertilize the ground for your own deliverance.

All things change and we cannot live permanently amid obstructions. *Inguz* signals your emergence from a closed, chrysalis state. As you resolve and clear away the old, you will experience a release from tension and uncertainty.

You may be required to free yourself from a rut, habit or relationship; from some deep cultural or behavioral pattern, some activity that was quite proper to the self you are leaving behind. The period at or just before birth is often a dangerous one. Movement involves danger yet movement that is timely leads out of danger. Now it is time to enter the delivery room.

Another of the Cycle Runes, *Inguz* counsels preparation. Being centered and grounded, freeing yourself from all unwanted influences, and seeing the humor, you are indeed prepared to open yourself to the Will of Heaven, and can await your deliverance with calm certainty.

9
Eihwaz

Defense

Avertive Powers

Yew Tree

As we are tested we fund the power to avert blockage and defeat. At the same time, we develop in ourselves an aversion to the conduct that creates stress in
our lives.

If there appears to be an obstacle in your path,
remember that even a delay may prove beneficial. Do
not be overly eager to press forward, for this is not a
situation in which you can make your influence felt.
Patience is the counsel *Eihwaz* offers: nothing hectic, no
acting needy, or lusting after a desired outcome. This
Rune speaks to the difficulties that arise at the beginning of new life. Often it announces a time of waiting—for a spring to fill up with water, for fruit to ripen
on the bough.

Perseverance and foresight are called for here. The
ability to foresee consequences before you act is a mark
of the profound person. Avert anticipated difficulties
through right action, this Rune is saying. For even more
than we are *doers,* we are *deciders.* And once the decision
is clear, the doing becomes effortless.

Receiving the Rune *Eihwaz,* you are put on notice that, through inconvenience and discomfort, growth is promoted. This may well be a trying time; certainly it is a meaningful one. As the wood of the yew tree becomes the bow of the Spiritual Warrior, so the obstacle on your path can become the gateway to a new life unfolding.

Set your house in order, tend to business, be clear, and wait on the Will of Heaven.

IO

Algiz

Protection

Sedge or Rushes

An Elk

Control of the emotions is at issue here. During times of transition, shifts in life course and accelerated self-change, it is important not to collapse yourself into your emotions—the highs as well as the lows. New opportunities and challenges are typical of this Rune. And with them will come trespasses and unwanted influences.

Algiz serves as a mirror for the Spiritual Warrior, the one whose battle is always with the self. The protection of the Warrior is like the warning rustle of the sedge grass or like the curved horns of the elk, for both serve to keep open space around you. Remain mindful that timely action and correct conduct are the only true protection. If you find yourself feeling pain, observe the pain, stay with it. Don't try to pull down the veil and escape from life by denying what is happening. You *will* progress; knowing that is your protection.

Reversed: Be thoughtful about your health and do not add to the burdens others are carrying. Look carefully at all associations you form at this time. If you see fit to become involved with people who are "using" you, remain conscious of that fact and take responsibility for your own position; then you can only benefit. Regardless of whether your enterprise prospers or suffers, do not be concerned: You may not win, but you will never lose, for you will always learn from what takes place. Temperance and courtesy are the sinews of this Rune's protective powers.

II

Fehu

Possessions

Nourishment

Cattle

Fehu is a Rune of fulfillment: ambition satisfied, love fulfilled, rewards received. It promises nourishment, from the most worldly to the sacred and Divine. For if the ancient principle "As above so below" is true, then we are also here to nourish God.

This Rune calls for a deep probing of the meaning of profit and gain in your life. Look with care to know whether it is wealth and possessions you require for your well-being, or rather self-rule and the growth of a will.

Another concern of *Fehu* is with conserving what has already been gained. It urges vigilance and continual mindfulness, especially in times of good fortune, for it is then that we are likely to collapse ourselves into our success on the one hand, or to behave recklessly on the other. Enjoy your good fortune and remember to share it; the mark of a well-nourished self is the willingness to nourish others.

 Reversed: There may be considerable frustration

in your life if you draw *Fehu Reversed,* a wide range of dispossessions reaching from the trivial to the severe. You fall short in your efforts, you reach out and miss, you watch helplessly while what you've gained dwindles away. Observe what is happening. Examine these events from an open perspective and ask, "What lesson do I need to learn from this in my life?"

Even if there is occasion for joy, do not let yourself be seduced into mindless joyousness. Reversed, this Rune indicates that doubtful situations are abundant and come in many forms and guises. You are being put in touch with the shadow side of possessions. Yet all this is part of the coming to be and passing away, and not that which abides. In dealing with the shadow side of *Fehu,* you have an opportunity to recognize where your true nourishment lies.

12

Wunjo

Joy

Light

This Rune is a fruit-bearing branch. The term of travail is ended and you have come to yourself in some regard. The shift that was due has occurred and now you can freely receive *Wunjo's* blessings, whether they be in material gain, in your emotional life or in a heightened sense of your own well-being. This is an alchemical moment in which understanding is transmuted from knowledge. The knowledge itself was a necessary but not sufficient condition; now you can rejoice, having been carried across the gap by the Will of Heaven.

Joyousness accompanies new energy, energy blocked before now. Light pierces the clouds and touches the waters just as something lovely emerges from the depths: The soul is illuminated from within, at the meeting place of Heaven and Earth, the meeting of the waters.

There is a new clarity which may call for you to renounce existing plans, ambitions, goals. It is proper and timely that you submit, for *Wunjo* is a Rune of restoration, of the self properly aligned to the Self.

Reversed: Things are slow in coming to fruition. The process of birth is long and arduous, and fears arise for the safety of the "child" within. A crisis, a difficult passage—even if brief—is at hand. Consideration and deliberation are called for. Ask yourself whether you possess the virtues of seriousness, sincerity and emptiness; to possess them is to have tranquility which is the ground for clarity, patience and perseverance.

Seen in its true light, *everything is a test.* And so, focused in the present, sincere toward others and trusting in your process, know that you cannot fail.

In times of crisis, this Rune Reversed is a useful meditation.

13
Jera

Harvest
Fertile Season
One Year

A Rune of beneficial outcomes, *Jera* applies to any activity or endeavor to which you are committed. Be aware, however, that no quick results can be expected. A span of time is always involved; hence the key words "one year," symbolizing a full cycle before the reaping, the harvest or deliverance.

You have prepared the ground and planted the seed. Now you must cultivate with care. To those whose labor has a long season, a long coming to term, *Jera* offers encouragement of success. Know that the outcome is in the keeping of Providence and continue to persevere.

Remember the old story about the farmer who was so eager to assist his crops that he went out at night and tugged on the new shoots. There is no way to push the river; equally you cannot hasten the harvest. Be mindful that patience is essential for the recognition of your own process which, in its season, leads to the harvest of the self.

Opening
Fire
Torch

This is the Rune of opening, renewed clarity, dispelling the darkness that has been shrouding some part of your life. You are free now to receive, and to know the joy of non-attached giving.

Kano is the Rune for the morning of activities, for seriousness, clear intent and concentration, all of which are essential at the beginning of work. The protection offered by *Kano* is this: The more Light you have, the better you can see what is trivial and outmoded in your conditioning.

In relationships, there can now be a mutual opening up. You may serve as the trigger, the timekeeper, through your awareness that the Light of understanding is once again available to you both.

Recognize that while on the one hand you are limited and dependent, on the other you exist at the perfect center where the harmonious and beneficent forces of the universe merge and radiate. You *are* that center.

Simply put, if you have been operating in the dark,

there is now enough light to see that the patient on the operating table is yourself.

Reversed: Expect a darkening of the light in some situation or relationship. A friendship may be dying, a partnership, a marriage, some aspect of yourself that is no longer appropriate to the person you are now. Receiving this Rune puts you on notice that failure to face up to the death consciously would constitute a loss of opportunity. *Kano* is one of the Cycle Runes. Reversed, it points to the death of a way of life invalidated by growth.

Reversed, this Rune calls for giving up gladly the old, and being prepared to live for a time empty: It calls for developing inner stability—not being seduced by the momentum of old ways while waiting for the new to become illuminated in its proper time.

Warrior Energy
The Sky God Tīw

This is the Rune of the Spiritual Warrior. Always the battle of the Spiritual Warrior is with the self. Funding a will through action, yet unattached to outcomes, remaining mindful that all you can really do is stay out of your own way and let the Will of Heaven flow through you—these are among the hallmarks of the Spiritual Warrior.

Embodied in this Rune is the sword of discrimination that enables you to cut away the old, the dead, the extraneous. And yet, with *Teiwaz* comes certain knowledge that the universe always has the first move. Patience is the virtue of this Rune, and it recalls the words of St. Augustine that "the reward of patience is patience."

Here, you are asked to look within, to delve down to the foundations of your life itself. Only in so doing can you hope to deal with the deepest needs of your nature and to tap into your most profound resources. The molding of character is at issue when *Teiwaz* appears in your spread.

Associated with this Rune are the sun, masculine energy, the active principle. The urge toward conquest is prominent here, especially self-conquest, which is a lifelong pursuit and calls for awareness, single-mindedness and the willingness to undergo your passage with compassion and in total trust.

In issues of relationship, devotion to a cause, an idea or a path of conduct, the Warrior Rune counsels perseverance, although at times the kind of perseverance required is patience.

Teiwaz is a Rune of courage and dedication. In ancient times it was this glyph warriors painted on their shields before battle. Now, the same symbol strengthens your resolve in the struggle of the Self with self.

Reversed: The danger is that through hasty or ill-timed action, life force leaks out or is spilled away. If an association is short-lived, do not grieve, but know that it has fulfilled its span. Matters of trust and confidence are at issue here, and with them the authenticity of your way of being in the world.

Reversed, *Teiwaz* calls for examining your motives. Is it self-conquest with which you are concerned, or are you trying to dominate another? Are you lusting after outcomes, or are you focused on the task for its own sake?

You will find the answers within yourself, not in outside advice. When you consult the Runes, you are consulting the Self, the action proper to a Spiritual Warrior.

Growth

Rebirth

A BirchTree

Another of the Cycle Runes, *Berkana* denotes a form of fertility that fosters growth both symbolically and actually. The growth may occur in affairs of the world, family matters, one's relationship to one's Self or to the Divine.

A Rune that leads to blossoming and ripening, *Berkana* is concerned with the flow of beings into their new forms. Its action is gentle, penetrating, and pervasive.

What is called for here is going into things deeply, with care and awareness. First disperse resistance, then accomplish the work. For this to happen, your will must be clear and controlled, your motives correct. Any dark corners should be cleansed; this must be carried out diligently and sometimes with expert help. Modesty, patience, fairness and generosity are called for here. Once resistance is dispersed and rectification carried out and seen to hold firm, then, through steadfastness and right attitude, the blossoming can occur.

Reversed: Events or, more likely, aspects of character interfere with the growth of new life. You may feel dismay at failing to take right action. But rather than dismay, what is called for is diligence. Examine what has occurred, your role in it, your needs, the needs of others. Are you placing your *wants* before the *needs* of others? Strip away until you can identify the obstacles to growth in this situation. Then, penetrating gently, imitate the wind.

You may be required to fertilize the ground again, but through correct preparation, growth is assured.

Movement

Progress

A Horse

Ehwaz is a Rune of transit, transition and move-ment; of physical shifts, new dwelling places, new atti-tudes or new life. It also signifies movement in the sense of improving or bettering any situation.

There is about this Rune a sense of gradual devel-opment and steady progress, with the accompanying notion of slow growth through numerous shifts and changes. This could apply to the growth of a business or to the development of an idea. A relationship may need to undergo changes if it is to maintain growth and life. Moral effort and steadfastness are called for when you draw *Ehwaz,* another of the Cycle Runes. Let it be said this way: "As I cultivate my own nature, all else follows."

This Rune's symbol is the horse, and it signifies the inseparable bond between horse and rider. Bronze Age artifacts show a horse drawing the sun across the sky. Here, this Rune is saying, you have progressed far enough to feel a measure of safety in your position. It is time to turn again and face the future reassured, prepared to share the good fortune that comes. The sharing is significant since it relates to the sun's power to foster life and illuminate all things with its light.

[W] **Reversed:** Movement that appears to block. Be certain that what you are doing—or not doing—is timely. We have simply to recognize that not all opportunities are appropriate, that not all possibilities are open to us. The opportunity at hand may be precisely to avoid action. If you are feeling at a loss, unclear about the need to act, consider what is timely to your nature, and remember: What is yours will come to you.

Flow

Water

That Which Conducts

Unseen powers are active here, powers that nourish, shape and connect. The attributes of this Rune are water, fluidity, the ebb and flow of emotions, of vocations and relationships. *Laguz* fulfills your desire to immerse yourself in the experience of living without having to evaluate or understand. It speaks to the satisfaction of emotional needs, to the awakening of the intuitive or lunar side of your nature. For while the sun strives for differentiation, the moon draws us toward union and merging.

This Rune often signals a time for cleansing: for revaluing, reorganizing, realigning. A Rune of deep knowing, *Laguz* may call you to study spiritual matters in readiness for self-transformation. Success now lies in contacting your intuitive knowing, in attuning to your own rhythms. A Rune of the self relating rightly to the Self, *Laguz* signifies what alchemists called the *conjunctio,* or sacred marriage. In fairy tales, it is the end where the hero and heroine live happily ever after.

Reversed: A warning against overreach, excessive striving; a counsel against trying to exceed your own strength or operate beyond the power you have funded to date in your life.

Laguz Reversed often indicates a failure to draw upon the wisdom of instinct. As a result, the intuitive side of your nature may be languishing, leaving you out of balance. What is called for now is to go within, to honor the receptive side of your Warrior Nature.

Disruptive Natural Forces
Elemental Power
Hail

Change, freedom, invention and liberation are all attributes of this Rune. Drawing it indicates a pressing need within the psyche to break free from constricting identification with material reality and to experience the world of archetypal mind.

The Rune of elemental disruption, of events that seem to be totally beyond your control, *Hagalaz* has only an upright position, and yet it always operates through reversal. When you draw this Rune, expect disruption, for it is the Great Awakener, although the form the awakening takes may vary. Perhaps you will experience a gradual feeling of coming to your senses, as though you were emerging from a long sleep. Then again, the onset of power may be such as to rip away the fabric of what you previously knew as your reality, your security, your understanding of yourself, your work, your relationships or beliefs.

Be aware, however, that what operates here is not ultimately an outside force, not a situation of you-at-the-mercy-of-externals. Your own nature is creating what is happening, and you are not without power. The inner strength you have funded until now in your life is your support and guide at a time when everything you've taken for granted is being challenged.

The more severe the disruption in your life, the more significant and timely the requirements for your growth. Another of the Cycle Runes, the term "radical discontinuity" best describes the action of *Hagalaz* at its most forceful. The universe and your own soul are demanding that you do, indeed, grow.

A Journey
Communication
Union, Reunion

This Rune is concerned with communication, with the attunement of something that has two sides, two elements, and with the ultimate reunion that comes at the end of the journey, when what is above and what is below are united and of one mind.

Inner worth mounts here, and at such a time you must remember that you are not intended to rely entirely upon your own power, but rather to ask what constitutes *right action*. Ask through prayer, through addressing your own knowing, the Witness Self, the Teacher Within. Not intent on movement, be content to wait; while you wait, keep on removing resistances. As the obstructions give way, all remorse arising from "trying to make it happen" disappears.

The Journey is toward self-healing, self-change and union. You are concerned here with nothing less than unobstructed, perfect union. But the Union of Heaven and Earth cannot be forced. Regulate any excesses in your life. Material advantages must not weigh heavily on this Journey of the self toward the Self.

124

Stand apart even from like-minded others; the notion of strength in numbers does not apply at this time, for this part of the journey cannot be shared.

Another of the Cycle Runes, *Raido* represents the soul's journey and has within it the element of Joy, for the end is in sight. No longer burdened by what you've left behind, Heaven above you and the Earth below you unite within you and support you on your way.

A simple prayer for the soul's journey is:

I will to will Thy Will.

Reversed: Receiving this Rune Reversed puts you on notice to be particularly attentive to personal relationships. At this time, ruptures are more likely than reconciliations. Effort will be required to keep your good humor. Whatever happens, how you respond is up to you.

The requirements of your process may totally disrupt what you had intended. Hoped-for outcomes may elude you. And yet what you regard as detours, inconveniences, disruptions, obstacles and even failures and deaths will actually be *rerouting opportunities,* with union and reunion as the only abiding destinations.

Gateway
Place of Non-Action
The God Thor

With a gateway for its symbol, this Rune indicates that there is work to be done both inside and outside yourself. The gateway is the frontier between Heaven and the mundane. Arriving here is a recognition of your readiness to contact the numinous, the Divine, to illuminate your experience so that its meaning shines through its form.

Thurisaz is a Rune of non-action. Thus, the gateway is not to be approached and passed through without contemplation. Here you are being confronted with a true reflection of what is hidden in yourself, what must be exposed and examined before successful action can be undertaken. This Rune strengthens your ability to wait. Now is not a time to make decisions. Deep transformational forces are at work in this next-to-last of the Cycle Runes.

Visualize yourself standing before a gateway on a hilltop. Your entire life lies out behind you and below. Before you step through, pause and review the past: the learning and the joys, the victories and the sorrows—

everything it took to bring you here. Observe it all, bless it all, release it all. For in letting go of the past you reclaim your power.

Step through the gateway now.

Reversed: A quickening of your development is indicated here. And yet even when the growth process accelerates, you will have reason to halt along the way, to reconsider the old, to integrate the new. Take advantage of these halts.

If you are undergoing difficulties, remember: The quality of your passage depends upon your attitude and upon the clarity of your intention. Be certain that you are not suffering over your suffering.

Drawing *Thurisaz Reversed* demands contemplation on your part. Hasty decisions at this time may cause regrets, for the probability is that you will act from weakness, deceive yourself about your motives and create new problems more severe than those you are attempting to resolve. Impulses must be tempered by thought for correct procedure. *Do not attempt to go beyond where you haven't yet begun.* Be still, collect yourself, and wait on the Will of Heaven.

Breakthrough
Transformation
Day

Here is the final Rune belonging to the Cycle of Initiation. Drawing *Dagaz* marks a major shift or break-through in the process of self-change, a complete transformation in attitude—a 180-degree turn. For some, the transition is so radical that they no longer continue to live the ordinary life in the ordinary way.

Because the timing is right, the outcome is assured although not, from the present vantage point, predictable. In each life there comes at least one moment which, if recognized and seized, transforms the course of that life forever. Rely, therefore, on radical trust, even though the moment may call for you to leap, empty-handed into the void. With this Rune your Warrior Nature reveals itself.

If *Dagaz* is followed by the Blank Rune, the magnitude of the transformation might be so total as to portend a death, the successful conclusion to your passage.

A major period of achievement and prosperity is often introduced by this Rune. The darkness is behind you; daylight has come. However, as always, you are reminded not to collapse yourself into the future or to behave recklessly in your new situation. A lot of hard work can be involved in a time of transformation. Undertake to do it joyfully.

Standstill
That Which Impedes
Ice

The winter of the spiritual life is upon you. You may find yourself entangled in a situation to whose implications you are, in effect, blind. You may be powerless to do anything except submit, surrender, even sacrifice some long-cherished desire. Be patient, for this is the period of gestation that precedes a rebirth.

Positive accomplishment is unlikely now. There is a freeze on useful activity, all your plans are on hold. You may be experiencing an unaccustomed drain on your energy and wonder why: A chill wind is reaching you over the ice floes of old outmoded habits.

Trying to hold on can result in shallowness of feeling, a sense of being out of touch with life. Seek to discover what it is you are holding onto that keeps this condition in effect, and let go. Shed, release, cleanse away the old. That will bring on the thaw.

Usually *Isa* requires a sacrifice of the personal, the "I." And yet there is no reason for anxiety. Submit and be still, for what you are experiencing is not necessarily the result of your actions or habits, but of the conditions of the time against which you can do nothing. What has been full must empty; what has increased must decrease. This is the way of Heaven and Earth. To surrender is to display courage and wisdom.

At such a time, do not hope to rely on help or friendly support. In your isolation, exercise caution and do not stubbornly persist in attempting to work your will. Remain mindful that the seed of the new is present in the shell of the old, the seed of unrealized potential, the seed of the good. Trust your own process, and watch for signs of spring.

Wholeness

Life Forces

The Sun's Energy

This Rune stands for Wholeness, that which your nature requires. It embodies the impulse toward self-realization and indicates the path you must follow, not from ulterior motives but from the core of your individuality.

Seeking after Wholeness is the Spiritual Warrior's quest. And yet what you are striving to become in actuality is what you, by nature, already are. You must become conscious of your essence and bring it into form, express it in a creative way. A Rune of great power, making life force available to you, *Sowelu* marks a time for regeneration right down to the cellular level.

Although this Rune has no Reversed position, there is reason for caution. You may see fit to withdraw, to retreat in the face of a pressing situation, especially if events or people are demanding that you expend your energy now. Know that such a retreat is a retreat in strength, and that it can indicate the need for a voyage inward for centering, for balance. Timely retreat is among the skills of the Spiritual Warrior.

At the same time, for some this Rune counsels opening yourself up, letting the Light into a part of your life that has been secret, shut away. To accomplish this may call for profound recognitions, for admitting to yourself something that you have long denied.

There is a prayer known as the *Gayatri* that embodies the spirit of *Sowelu*. Address the sun in this fashion:

> *You, who are the source of all power,*
> *Whose rays illuminate the whole world,*
> *Illuminate also my heart*
> *So that it too can do Your work.*

While reciting the *Gayatri*, visualize the sun's rays streaming forth into the world, entering your own heart, and then streaming out from your heart center, back into the world. This is a powerful and life-enhancing prayer.

Again, there is a caution here not to give yourself airs. Even in a time of bountiful energy, you are required to face and vanquish your refusal to let right action flow through you. Nourish this capacity, for it is a mark of true humility.

Practice the art of doing without doing: Aim yourself truly and then maintain your aim without manipulative effort. For by our own power we do nothing. Even in loving, it is Love that loves through us. This way of thinking and being integrates new energies and permits you to flow into Wholeness, which is the ultimate goal of the Spiritual Warrior.

The Unknowable
The God Odin

Blank is the end, blank the beginning. This is the Rune of total trust and should be taken as exciting evidence of your most immediate contact with your own true destiny which, time and again, rises like the phoenix from the ashes of what we call fate.

The *Blank Rune* can portend a death. But that death is usually symbolic, and may relate to any part of your life as you are living it now. *Relinquishing control is the ultimate challenge for the Spiritual Warrior.*

Here the Unknowable informs you that it is in motion in your life. In that blankness is held undiluted potential. At the same time both pregnant and empty, it comprehends the totality of being, all that is to be actualized. And if, indeed, there are "matters hidden by the gods," you need only remember: What beckons is the creative power of the unknown.

Drawing the *Blank Rune* brings to the surface your deepest fears: Will I fail? Will I be abandoned? Will it all be taken away? And yet your highest good, your truest possibilities and all your fertile dreams are held within that blankness.

Willingness and permitting are what this Rune requires, for how can you exercise control over what is not yet in form? The *Blank Rune* often calls for no less an act of courage than the empty-handed leap into the void. Drawing it is a direct test of Faith.

The *Blank Rune* represents the path of *karma*—the sum total of your actions and of their consequences. At the same time, this Rune teaches that the very debts of old karma shift and evolve as you shift and evolve. *Nothing is predestined:* The obstacles of your past can become the gateways that lead to new beginnings.

Whenever you draw the *Blank Rune,* take heart: Know that the work of self-change is progressing in your life.

I no longer try to change outer things. They are simply a reflection. I change my inner perception and the outer reveals the beauty so long obscured by my own attitude. I concentrate on my inner vision and find my outer view transformed. I find myself attuned to the grandeur of life and in unison with the perfect order of the universe.

—Daily Word

Warrior Horseman, Mjoboro,
Uppland, Sweden, sixth century

8

THEATER
OF THE SELF

*We are all teachers, and what we teach is what we need to learn, and
so we teach it over and over again until we learn it.*

—A principle of *A Course in Miracles*

Almost five months after establishing the order
and meaning of the Runes, while driving south along
the Pacific Coast Highway, I had a strong feeling about
the interrelated sequence of the Runes. I suddenly understood that each Rune is linked to the next through
a progressive development which represents the
twenty-five steps of the self growing into wholeness.

Without bothering to pull off the road, I opened
my Rune notes and, starting with *Mannaz,* the Rune of
the Self, jotted down the essential meaning for each
Rune as it connected it to its neighbor. I wrote steadily
as I drove, still in the fast lane, using the steering wheel
as my table while glancing between the page and the
highway. The miles passed by and all the connections
flowed into place. I was just coming to the Blank Rune
when I caught a movement out of my right eye. Beyond

the car window and staring at me with an expression that said "I don't believe this!" was a California highway patrolman on his motorcycle. My speedometer registered 72 mph. We both pulled over. I didn't even try to explain.

At the roadside, I completed my notes. When I returned home I recopied what I had written, observing its pattern, listening to its rhythm. Not only did the progression hold, it fell into five clusters or acts. Here then are The Viking Runes, divided into Five Acts, in the play of the self coming to the Self.

Act I: The starting point is the self [M] which, in its willingness to change, undertakes Partnership [X] at the highest level—Partnership with the Divine—and in so doing receives the Gift of freedom. The self is assisted in its urge to grow by the Messenger Rune [ᚠ], which operates between the Divine and the self through Signals in the form of new connections that lead into new pathways. During this process, there occurs a peeling away, a shedding of old skins that brings about Separation and Retreat [ᛉ] and loosens the bonds you have inherited from being in the world. Once this transformation is underway, Strength [ᚢ] becomes available for growth into Manhood and Womanhood.

Act II: This is the moment of Initiation [ᛕ] when release of the old leads to new wholeness. The process occurs on an inner level and nothing external matters here. Next, the self undergoes the Pain of Necessary

Constraint ⊬ in order to be cleansed and healed, for rectification precedes progress. Out of the cleansing comes Fertility, New Beginnings ᛝ . Since the new creature is totally vulnerable, Defense ᛇ is provided: Through being tested you develop the power to avoid self-injury. This Rune is followed by another more positive form of Protection ᛉ , which calls for correct conduct and timely action. To progress well is the best protection.

Act III: Now the self can receive the Nourishment ᚠ it requires, either in the form of Possessions or through the achievement of well-being and self-rule. This brings Joy and Happiness ᚹ from within, a sense of having come to oneself. There follows a period of waiting for the Harvest ᛃ , a time marked by patience and perseverance, and a time of careful cultivation until, at the harvest time, the self experiences an Opening Up ᚲ , new Light in which both to receive and to know the joy of giving. This new Light reveals the birth of the Spiritual Warrior ᛏ , the one who possesses the sword of discrimination that cuts away the old outgrown life. With the birth of the Spiritual Warrior, we arrive at the Third Act curtain, the essential midpoint of our journey.

Act IV: As the Spiritual Warrior pursues the path with a heart, Growth ᛒ is the main concern. There is no urge to turn back. The self is more centered, better prepared when, with Movement ᛗ , changes and progress come; for as you cultivate your nature, all else follows. With the help of Water, That Which Conducts ⑂ , another cleansing and balancing occurs. Now the self is prepared for the upsurge of Natural Forces ⑂ , forces that disrupt it totally as old outmoded habits fall away. At last, a new synthesis is possible, marked by Communication ⑂, a Journey toward Reunion with the Higher Self on the path toward Union with the Divine.

Act V: The path stretches upward, climbing to a Gateway ⑂ , a place of Non-Action calling for meditation on the progress so far. Integration is the hallmark of this, a second stage of Initiation. For beyond the Gateway lies a major Breakthrough, a Transformation ⑂ signified by radical trust and a leap of Faith. Then everything comes to standstill ⑂ until, out of that ice-bound stage the Sun, Life Force ⑂, liberates new energies, a new way of being. And finally, the Spiritual Warrior arrives at the Rune of All-in-All, the Blank Rune ⑂ , from whose emptiness comes again, in eternal renewal, the starting point for the self. . . .

At the end of Act V, the self is once more at the beginning, a new beginning.

THE GIFT OF THE SELF

There are no more maps, no more creeds, no more philosophies. From here on in, the directions come straight from the Divine. The Curriculum is being revealed millisecond by millisecond—invisibly, intuitively, spontaneously, lovingly. As one of Thomas Merton's monks has it, "Go into your cell and your cell will teach you everything there is to know." Your cell. Yourself.

—Akshara Noor

Stone Lion with runic graffiti, Piraeus, Greece

9

AFTERWORD:
MAGIC IN THE
PRESENT TENSE

God is alive, magic is afoot.

—Leonard Cohen

At our best, each of us is a channel through which God's wisdom flows, and we are sensitive to the inner guidance that provides us with the intuitive knowing we require. But life can be hard and difficult and we are not always clear. The channels that we are become blocked by fears, silted up with self-doubt. We do not always hear the still small voice that is our natural inheritance.

The Runes are available to be used as a bridge to your Knowing Self. While contemplating a Rune chosen to illuminate a particular issue, remain clear about one thing: *You are not depending on the Oracle to solve your problems for you.* Images and thoughts will come to mind, image-ideas that will provide you with the necessary clues as to what constitutes timely right action. Working with the Oracle in this way, you will fund a new sense of confidence, a new kind of courage.

The Viking Runes are a mirror for the magic of our Knowing Selves. In time, as you become skilled in their use, you can lay the Runes aside and permit the knowing to arise unfiltered, just as some dowsers use only their bare hands to find water.

Any Oracle is a reflection of the culture in which it evolves. The roots of the Tarot and the *I Ching* are not Western roots; the Tarot did not emerge into Western life until the Runes were more than 1,000 years old; the *I Ching* took another 800 years to reach the West. In the Runes we are provided with a symbolic system that derives from an Oracle arising within the forms of Western thought. It is both timely and providential that the Viking Runes once again be restored to service as a Western Oracle.

To all of you who have arrived at this place of termination and new beginnings, *Gud blessi thig.*

Bronze girdle ornament.
Birka, Sweden; ninth
century.

SELECTED BIBLIOGRAPHY

Bonner, W. "Survivals of Paganism in Anglo-Saxon England." *Transactions of the Birmingham Archaeological Society,* vol. 56, 1932.

Branston, B. *The Lost Gods of England.* London, 1957.

Dickens, B. "English Names and Old English Heathenism." *Essays and Studies,* vol. 19, 1934.

———. "Runic Rings and Old English Charms." *Archiv Stud. neuren Sprachen,* vol. 167, 1935.

———. "A System of Transliteration for Old English Runic Inscriptions." *Leeds Studies in English,* vol. 1, 1932.

Elliott, Ralph W. V. *Runes: An Introduction.* Manchester, Eng.: Manchester University Press, 1959.

———. "Runes, Yews, and Magic." *Speculum,* vol. 32, 1957.

Graham-Campbell, James. *Viking Artefacts, A Select Catalogue.* London: British Museum Publications Limited, 1980.

Grattan, J.H.G., and Singer, S. *Anglo-Saxon Magic and Medicine.* London, 1952.

Haugen, Einar. *The Scandinavian Languages.* Cambridge, Mass.: Harvard University Press, 1976.

Hermannsson, H. Catalogue of Runic Literature—Part of the Icelandic Collection Bequeathed by Willard Fiske. Cornell University Library.

Hollander, Lee M. *The Poetic Edda.* Austin: University of Texas Press, 1964.

Holmzvist, Wilhelm. *Swedish Vikings on Helgo and Birka.* Stockholm: Swedish Booksellers Association, 1979.

144

Howard, Michael. *The Magic of the Runes.* New York: Samuel Weiser, 1980.

———. *The Runes and Other Magical Alphabets.* Wellingborough, Northants, Eng.: Aquarian Press, 1978.

Jansson, Sven B. F. *The Runes of Sweden.* Translated by Peter Foote. London: Phoenix House, 1962.

Jones, Gwyn. *History of the Vikings.* London: Oxford University Press, 1968.

Knoop, Douglas, and Jones, G. P. *The Mediaeval Mason.* Manchester, Eng.: Manchester University Press, 1967.

Krause, Wolfgang. *Was Mann in Runen Ritzte.* Halle, Ger.: M. Niemeyer, 1935.

Lowe, Michael and Blacker, Carmen. *Oracles and Divination.* Boulder, CO: Shambhala, 1981.

Magnusson, Magnus. *Hammer of the North.* London: Orbis Publishing Limited, 1979.

Marstrander, C.J.S. "Om runene og runenavnenes oprindelse." *Norsk tidsskrift for sprogvidenskap,* vol. 1, 1928.

Napier, A. S. "The Franks Casket." *An English Miscellany Presented to Dr. Furnwall.* London: Oxford University Press, 1901.

Osborn, Marijane, and Longland, Stella. *Rune Games.* London: Routledge & Kegan Paul, Ltd., 1982.

Page, R. I. *An Introduction to English Runes,* London: Methuen, 1973.

Ravenscroft, Trevor. *The Spear of Destiny.* London: Neville Spearman, 1972.

Simpson, Jacqueline. *The Viking World.* New York: St. Martin's Press, 1980.

Souers, P. W. *Harvard Studies and Notes in Philology and Literature,* vol. 17, 1935; vol. 18, 1936; vol. 19, 1937.

Spiesberger, Karl. *Runenmagie, Handbuch der Runenkunde.* Berlin: Richard Schikowski, 1955.

Stephens, G. *Handbook of the Old-Northern Runic Monuments of Scandinavia and England.* London and Copenhagen, 1884.

———. *The Old-Northern Runic Monuments of Scandinavia and England.* London and Copenhagen, 1866–1901.

Storms, G. *Anglo-Saxon Magic.* The Hague, 1948.

Syversen, Earl. *Norse Runic Inscriptions with their Long-Forgotten Cryptography.* Sebastopol, CA., 1979.

Taylor, I. *Greeks and Goths: A Study on the Runes.* London, 1879.

Thompson, Claiborne W. *Studies in Upplandic Runography.* Austin: University of Texas Press, 1975.

Walgren, Erik. *The Kensington Rune Stone: A Mystery Solved.* Madison: University of Wisconsin Press, 1958.

Wilson, David. *The Vikings and their Origins.* London: Thames and Hudson Limited, 1970.

Wimmer, L.F.A. "Runeskriftens Oprindelse og Udvikling i Norden." *Aaboger for nordisk Oldkyndighed og Historie,* 1874.

PRONUNCIATION GUIDE

GERMANIC		SOUND VALUE OF THE GERMANIC AS IN MODERN ENGLISH
1. *Mannaz*	män-näz	*a* as in father
2. *Gebo*	gāy-bō	*e* as in play, *o* as in go
3. *Ansuz*	än-sōōz	*a* as in father, *u* as in ooze
4. *Othila*	ō-thē-lä	*o* as in go, *th* as in thin, *i* as in meet, *a* as in father
5. *Uruz*	ōō-rōōz	*u* as in ooze
6. *Perth*	perth	*e* as in berth
7. *Nauthiz*	now-thiz	*au* as in now, *th* as in thin, *i* as in is
8. *Inguz*	ing-gōōz	*ing* as in spring, *u* as in ooze
9. *Eihwaz*	ā-wäz	*ei* as in play, *a* as in father
10. *Algiz*	äl-gēz	*a* as in father, *g* as in gem, *i* as in meet
11. *Fehu*	fā-hew	*e* as in play, *u* as in hew

146

GERMANIC		SOUND VALUE OF THE GERMANIC AS IN MODERN ENGLISH
12. *Wunjo*	wōōn-jō	*u* as in wound, *j* as in joy, *o* as in go
13. *Jera*	jer-ä	*j* as in join, *e* as in yes, *a* as in father
14. *Kano*	kä-nō	*a* as in father, *o* as in go
15. *Teiwaz*	tā-wäz	*ei* as in play, *a* as in father
16. *Berkana*	ber-kä-nä	*e* as in berry, *a* as in father
17. *Ehwaz*	eh-wäz	*eh* as in yes, *a* as in father
18. *Laguz*	lä-gōōz	*a* as in father, *u* as in ooze
19. *Hagalaz*	hä-gä-läz	*a* as in father, *g* as in give
20. *Raido*	rī-thō	*ai* as in ride, *d* as in though, *o* as in go
21. *Thurisaz*	thu-ri-säz	*th* as in thin, *u* as in pull, *i* as in rip, *a* as in father
22. *Dagaz*	thä-gäz	*d* as in thin, *a* as in father
23. *Isa*	ē-sä	*i* as in easy, *a* as in father
24. *Sowelu*	sō-wāy-lōō	*o* as in go, *e* as in way, *u* as in ooze
25. *Odin*	ō-din	*o* as in go, *i* as in thin

THE RUNEWORKS

Using the Viking Runes has been, for many people, an exciting adventure of self-discovery. We would be most interested in hearing of *your* experiences with the Runes. Please feel encouraged to write to us at The RuneWorks.

We now need a way to establish better contact with each other and thereby stimulate further mutual growth along the path of the Spiritual Warrior. To this end, we publish a quarterly newsletter, *The New Oracle News & Rune Digest.* The newsletter serves as a forum for all of us to share our experiences with the Viking Runes. It contains information about other oracular traditions, innovations in Rune casting techniques, and new aspects of Rune play discovered by those who use the Oracle. We would like to quote from your letters; if you wish your name withheld, please let us know.

If you have difficulty finding *Rune Play* or *The Book of Runes,* or prefer to purchase additional copies (with or without stones) directly through us, please mail your inquiries to The RuneWorks.

In order to subscribe to *The New Oracle News & Rune Digest*, please write to:

> The RuneWorks
> P.O. Box 24084
> Los Angeles, CA 90024

We look forward to hearing from you.

Ralph Blum

ABOUT THE AUTHOR

Ralph Blum received his degree in Russian studies at Harvard. Following a period in Italy as a Fulbright Scholar, he returned to Harvard, where he did graduate work in anthropology with grants from the National Science Foundation and the Ford Foundation.

Encountering the Runes by chance while doing research in England, he subsequently explored their origins and reinterpreted their meanings in terms appropriate for our time. He is an anthropologist, writer, publisher and storyteller and has been working with the Viking Runes as a tool for self-counseling since 1978.

He makes his home in Malibu, California.

Silver cup from a royal grave. Jelling, Jutland, in Denmark; tenth century.

Futhark (*Traditional Order*)

MODERN ENGLISH EQUIVALENT	OLD ENGLISH RUNES	NAMES	GERMANIC RUNES	NAMES	ETRUSCAN	PRE-RUNIC SYMBOLS
f	ᚠ	feoh	ᚠ	fehu	ʎ	
u	ᚢ	ūr	ᚢ	ūruz	Υ V	△
þ (th)	ᚦ	þorn	ᚦ	þurisaz		
a	ᚫ	ōs	ᚨ	ansuz	A	
r	ᚱ	rād	ᚱ	raiðō	◁	
k	ᚻ	cēn	ᚲ	kaunaz kĕnaz kanō	> X	
g	ᚷ	gyfu	ᚷ	gebō		X
w	ᚹ	wyn	ᚹ	wunjō		
h	ᚻ	haegl	ᚺ	hagalaz	ᛒ	目
n	ᚾ	nȳð	ᚾ	nauþiz	Ϥ (ᚼ)	+
i	ᛁ	īs	ᛁ	īsa-	ᛁ	ᛁ
j	ᛄ	gēr	ᛃ	jēra-		↻
e (ei)	ᛇ	ēoh	ᛇ	eihwaz		⅏ ⅏
p	ᛈ	peorð	ᛈ	perþ	◁	
z	ᛉ	eolh-secg	ᛉ	algiz	I ‡	Υ ⅏
s	ᛋ	sigel	ᛋ	sowelu	⌇ ⌇	
t	↑	tīr	↑	teiwaz	T X	↑ ⇑
b	ᛒ	beorc	ᛒ	berkana-		
e	ᛖ	e(o)h	ᛖ	ehwaz	ᛄ	
m	ᛗ	man	ᛗ	mannaz	m ⅏	⌒
l	ᛚ	lagu	ᛚ	laguz	↓	
ng	ᛝ	Ing	☐	inguz	ⵚ	☐ ⵚ
o	ᛟ	eþel	ᛟ	oþila		X X
ð	ᛞ	daeg	ᛞ	ðagaz		ᛞ

Note: While the order of Rune names was to some degree fortuitous, the choice
names was not. A Rune name had to begin with a given sound and posse
mnemonic power